REST DAY:

A Mandatory Coloring Book

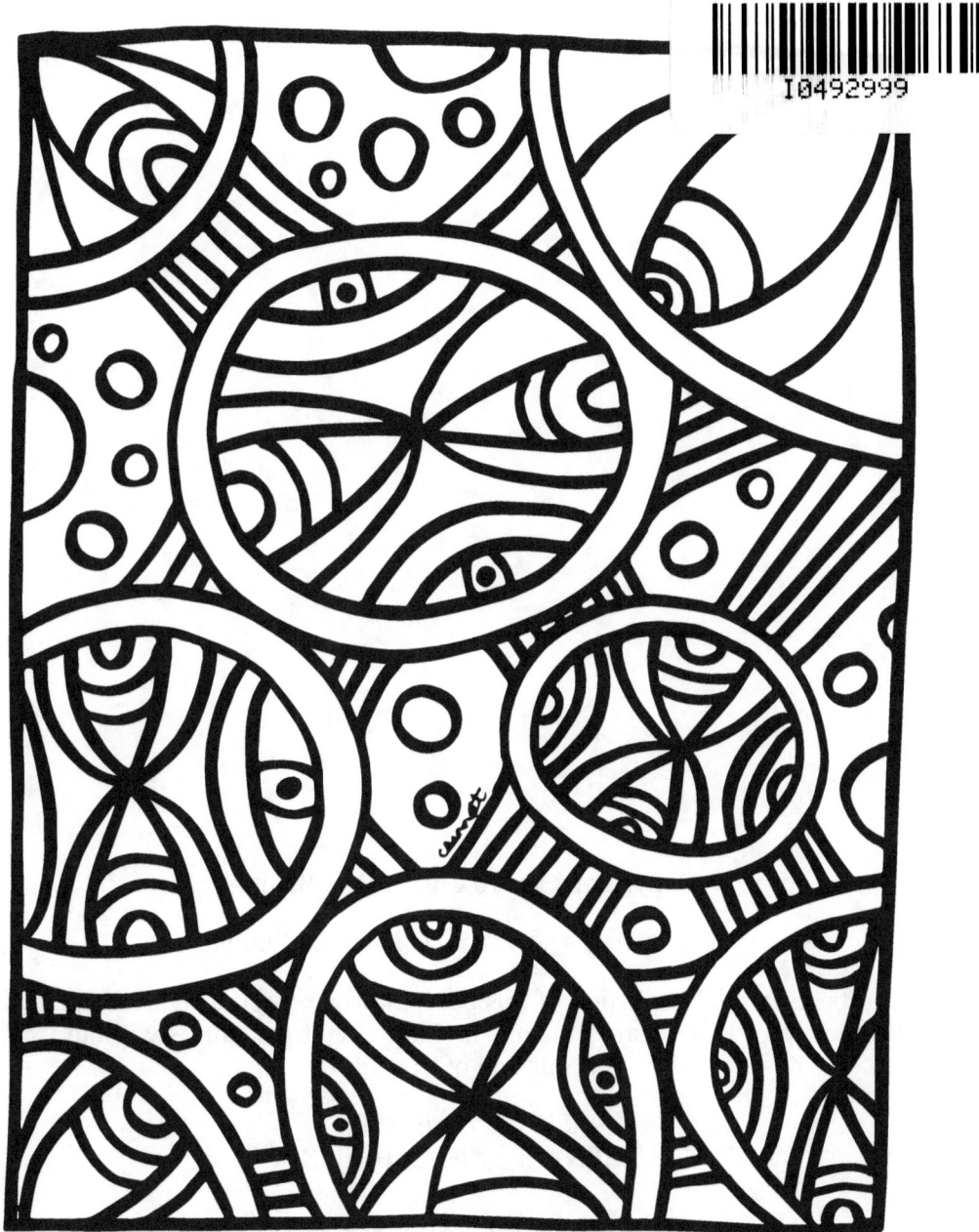

Christine S. Bennett

ISBN: **1534991182**
ISBN-13: **978-1534991187**

Printed in the United States of America.

First Printing July 2016.

This coloring book is dedicated to my husband Stuart.
Your support means everything.

Love you.

About this coloring book...

Love them or hate them, WE <u>ALL</u> NEED REST DAYS.

(To be perfectly honest...I don't like them). Gasp!

As a self-proclaimed fitness fanatic, I feel my day is incomplete without a good workout. For the longest time, I considered a 5-mile run as "rest". But, I know better...we all know better than that. We are doing a disservice to our bodies, and actually taking away from the progress we are seeking. Rest is an important part of the process that shouldn't be ignored.

So, whether you're a fitness fanatic, or a self proclaimed "workaholic", you need to make time to relax your mind and your body.

I'm a doodler...

Within the last year, I have tapped into my creativity through doodling. My doodles are spontaneous and random. I enjoy putting pen to paper and seeing what emerges. If you enjoy unique, hand-drawn designs, this book is for you!

The Rest Day coloring book...

I thought it would be fun to have a coloring book devoted to "rest days". So, I created 52 coloring pages that you can use as weekly reminders to recover and unwind.

Share YOUR Rest Day...

Share your Rest Day coloring page on social media, for a chance to be featured on my Facebook and/or Instagram pages! Just use the hash tag **#restdaybook .** I can't wait to see them!!

ENJOY!

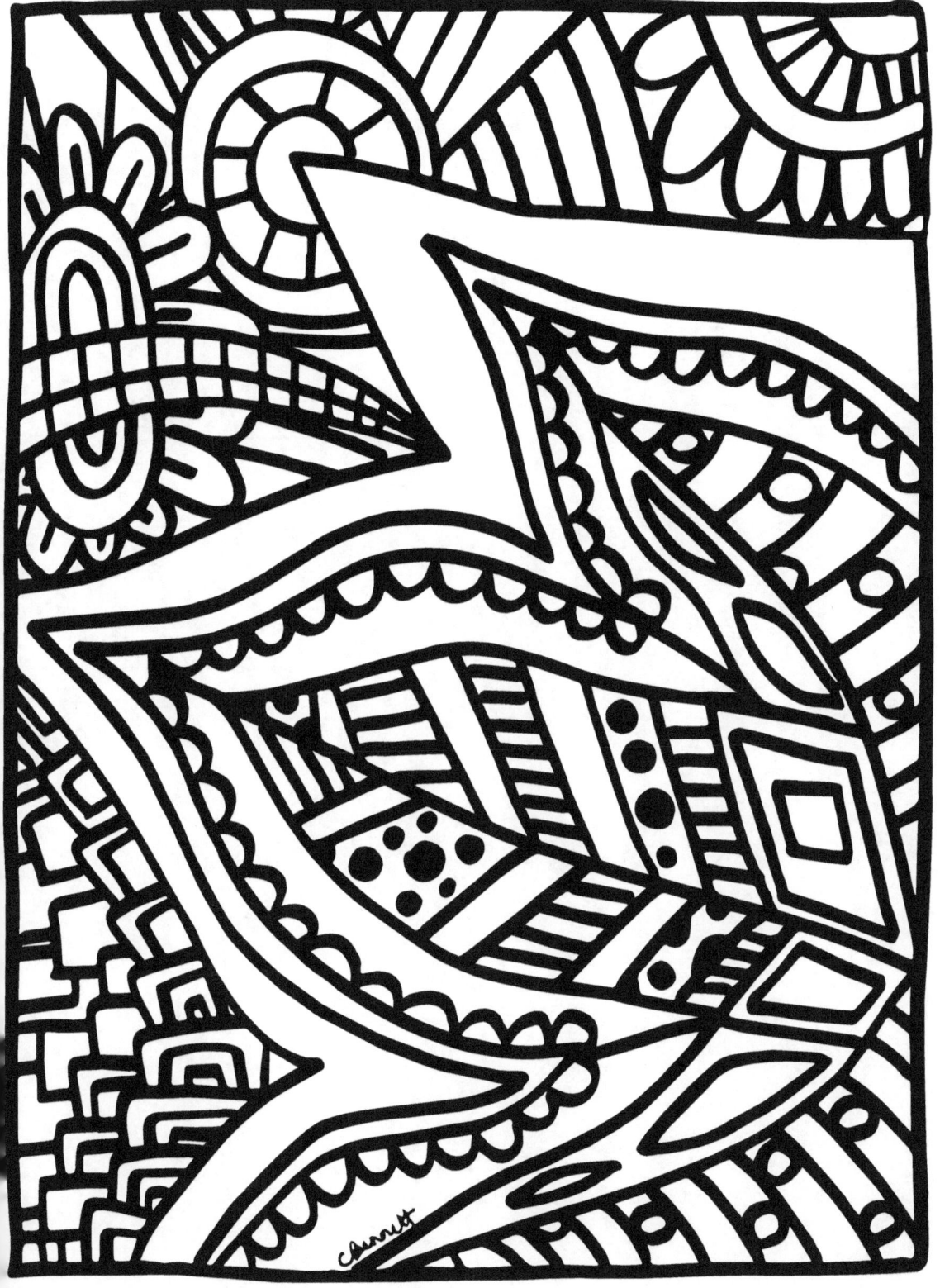

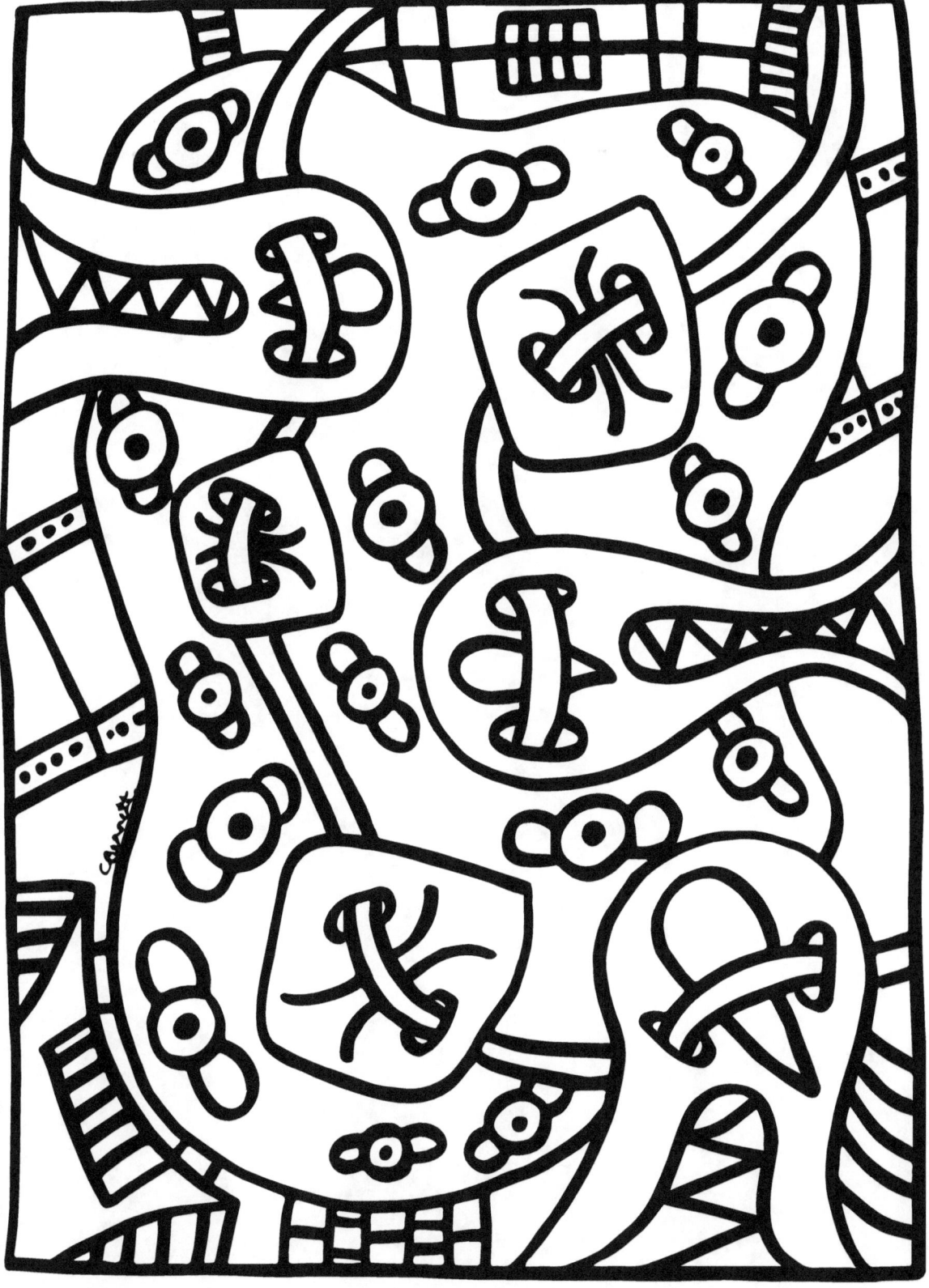

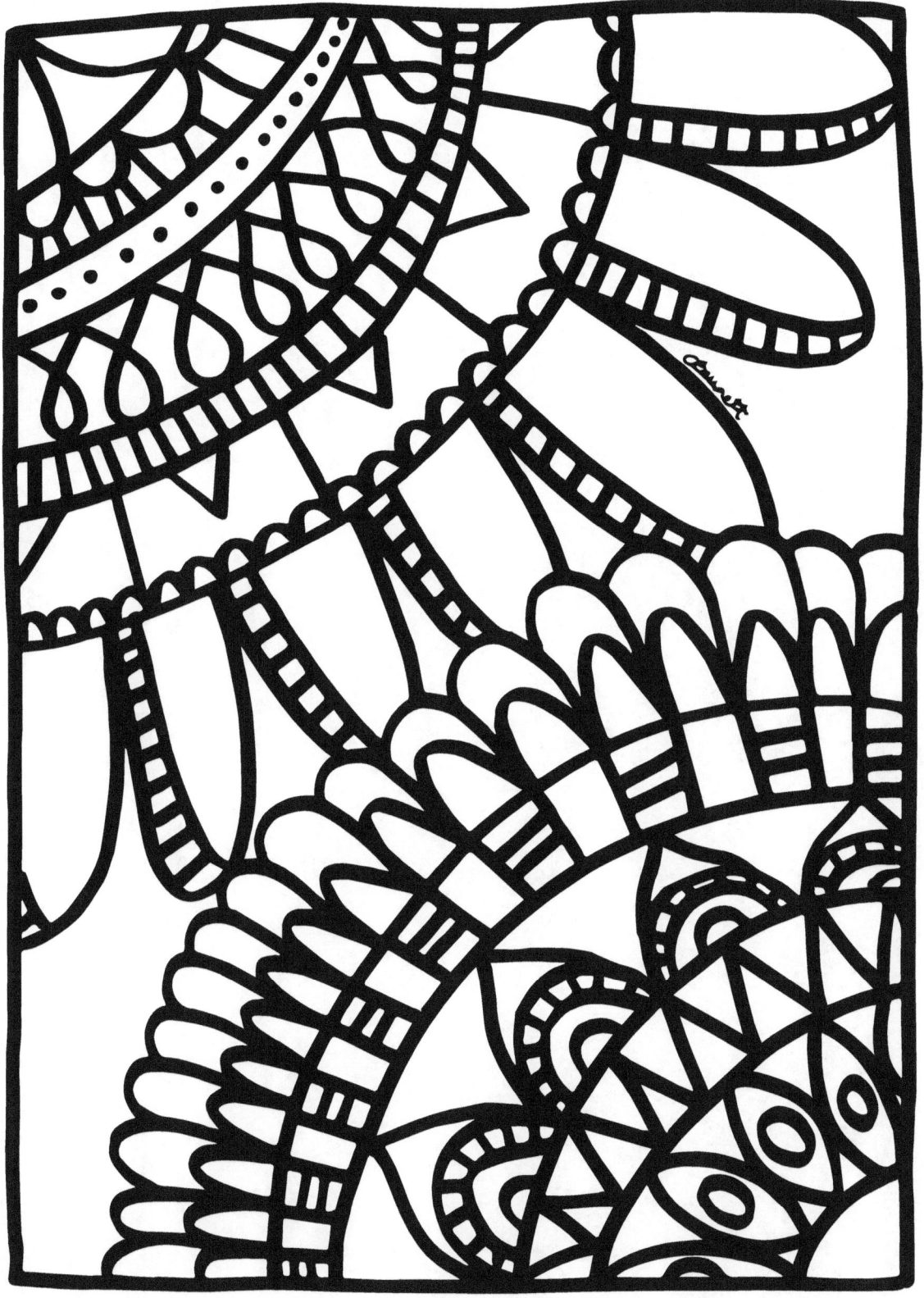

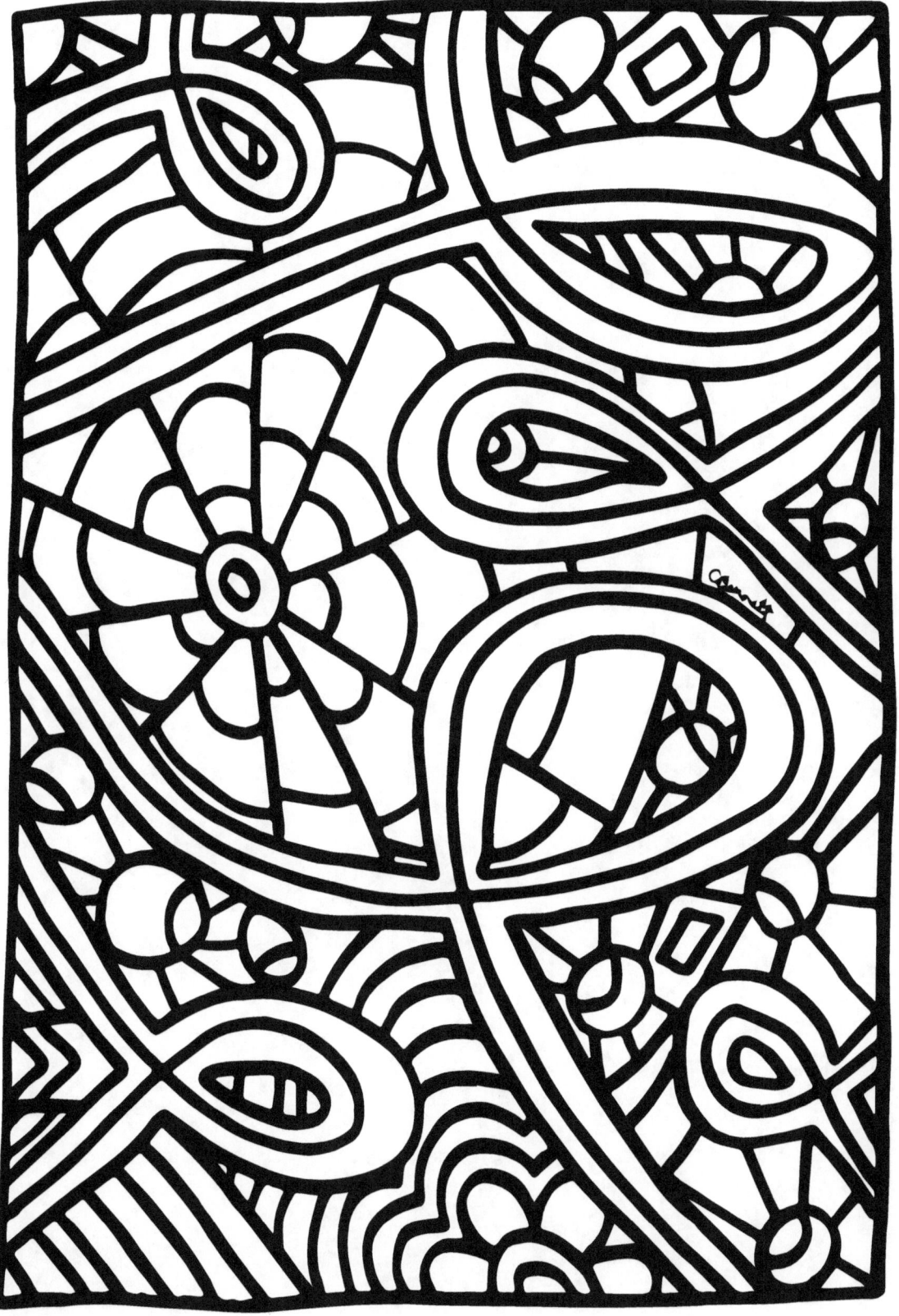

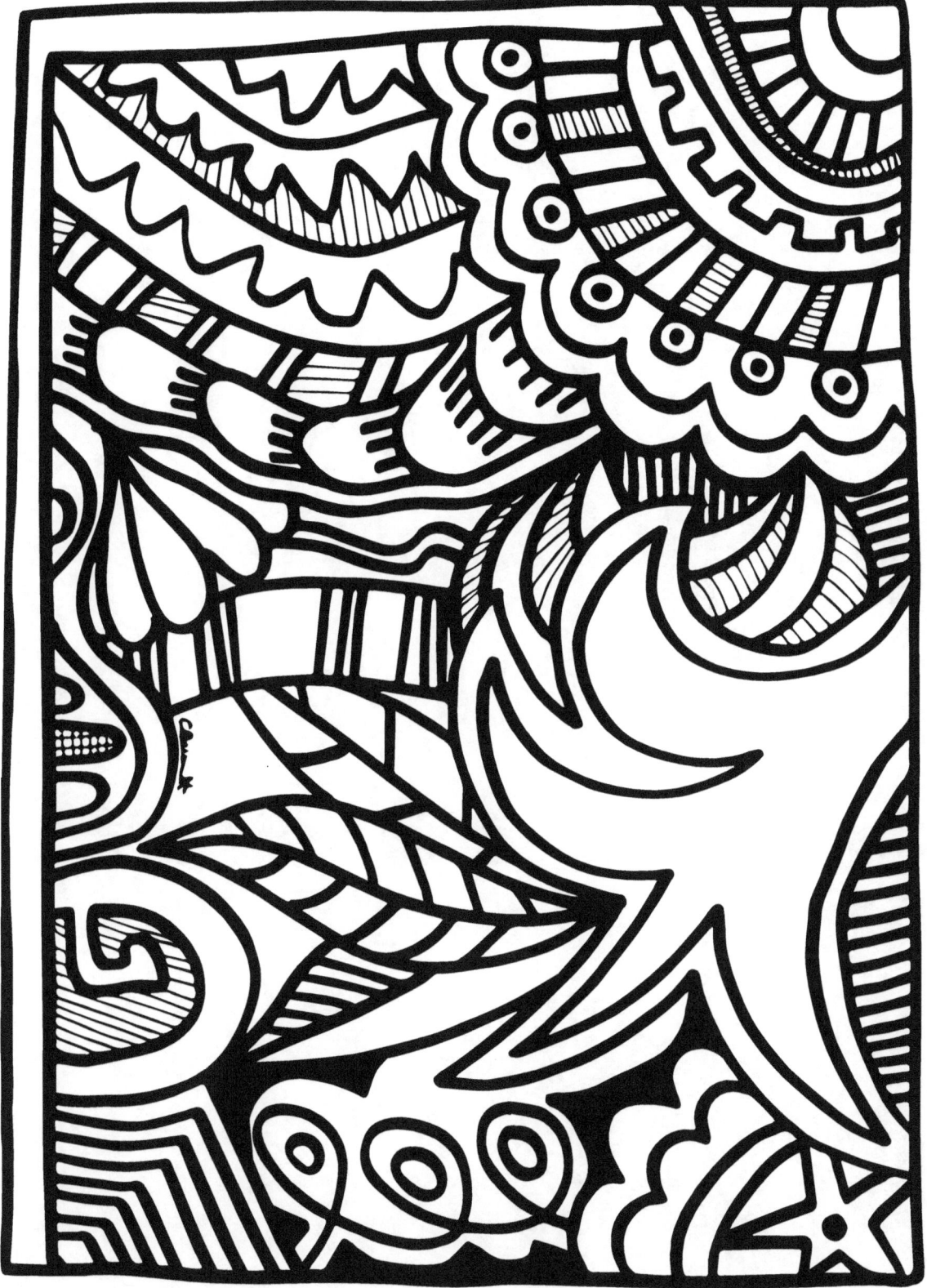

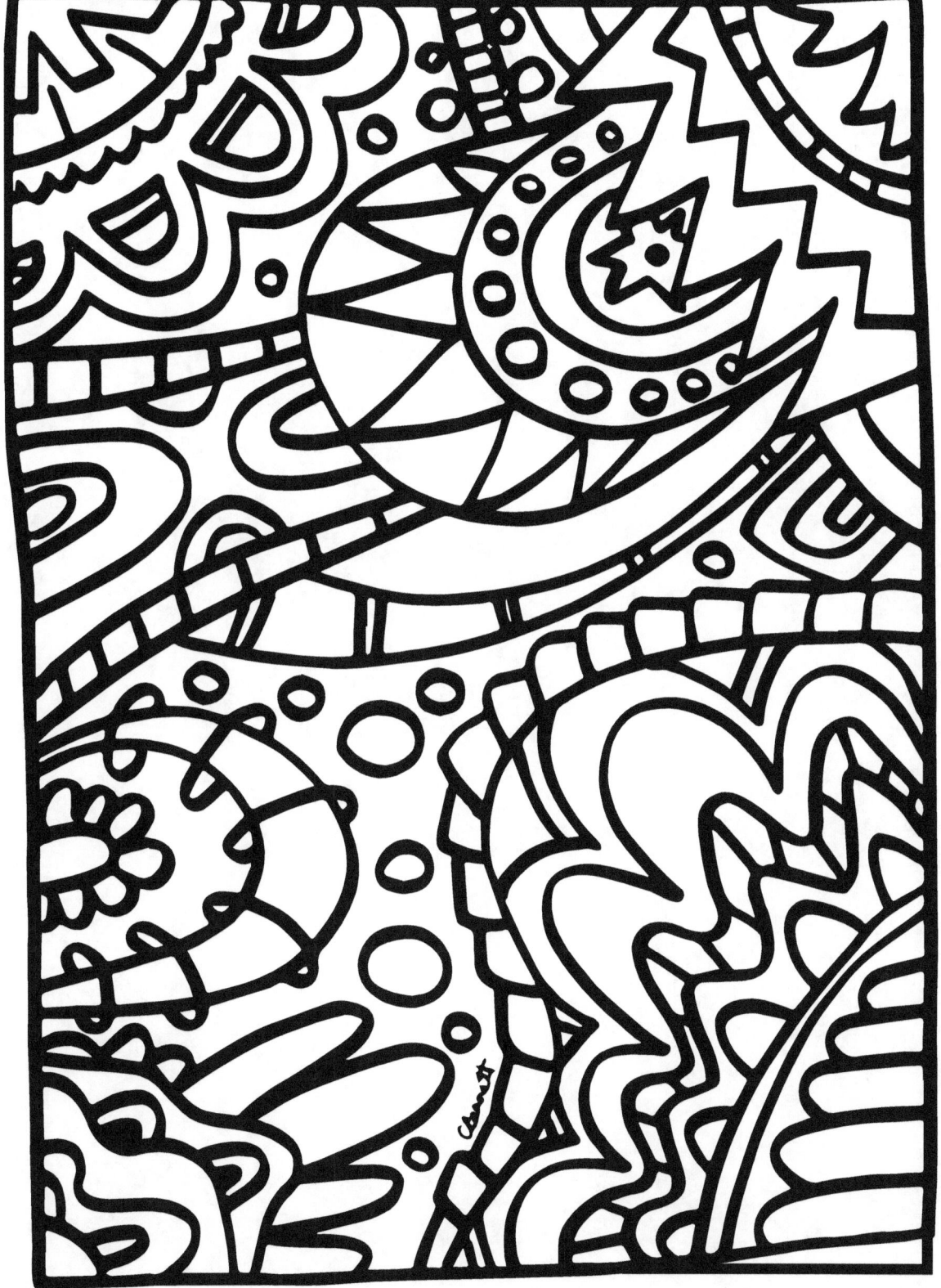

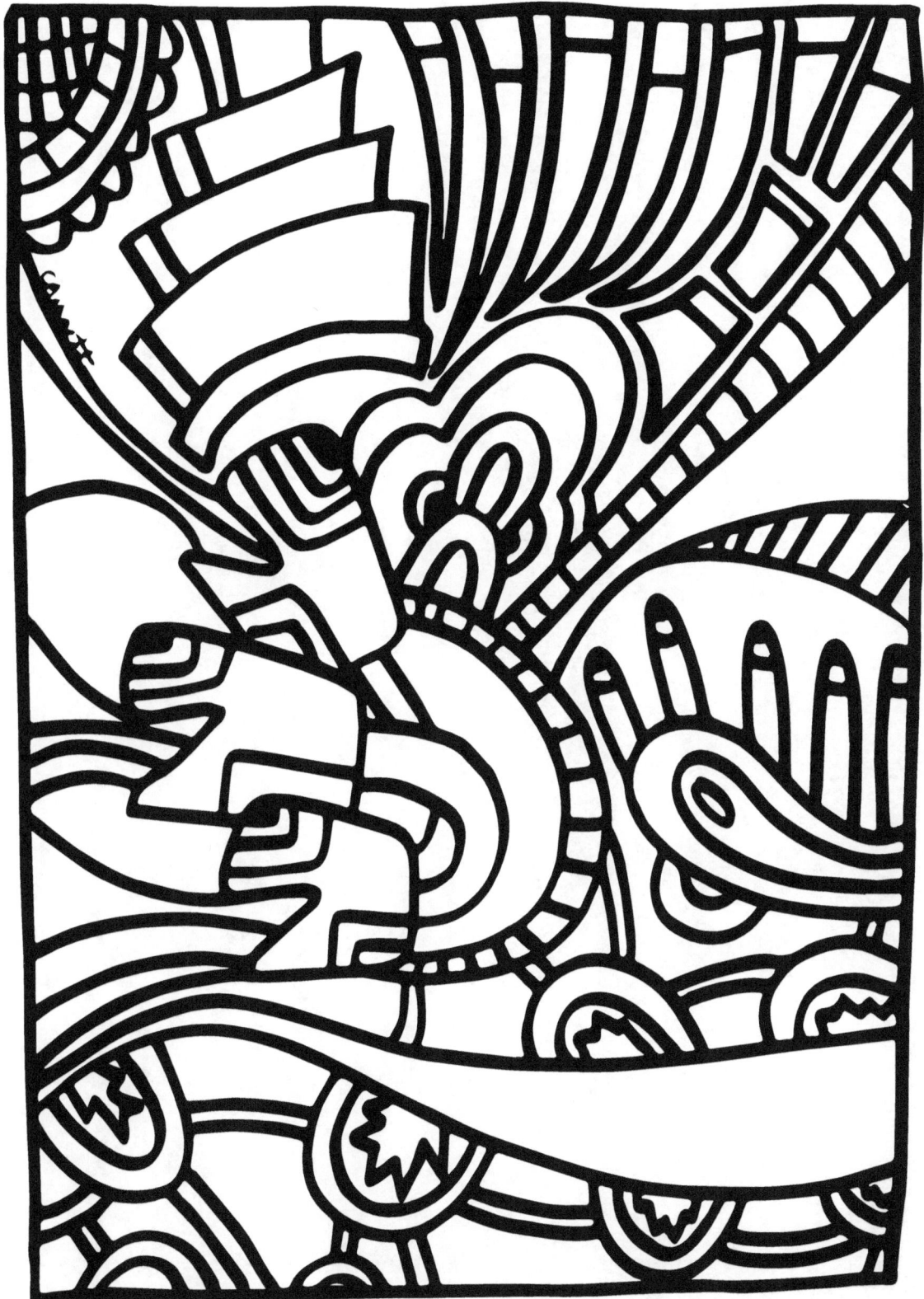

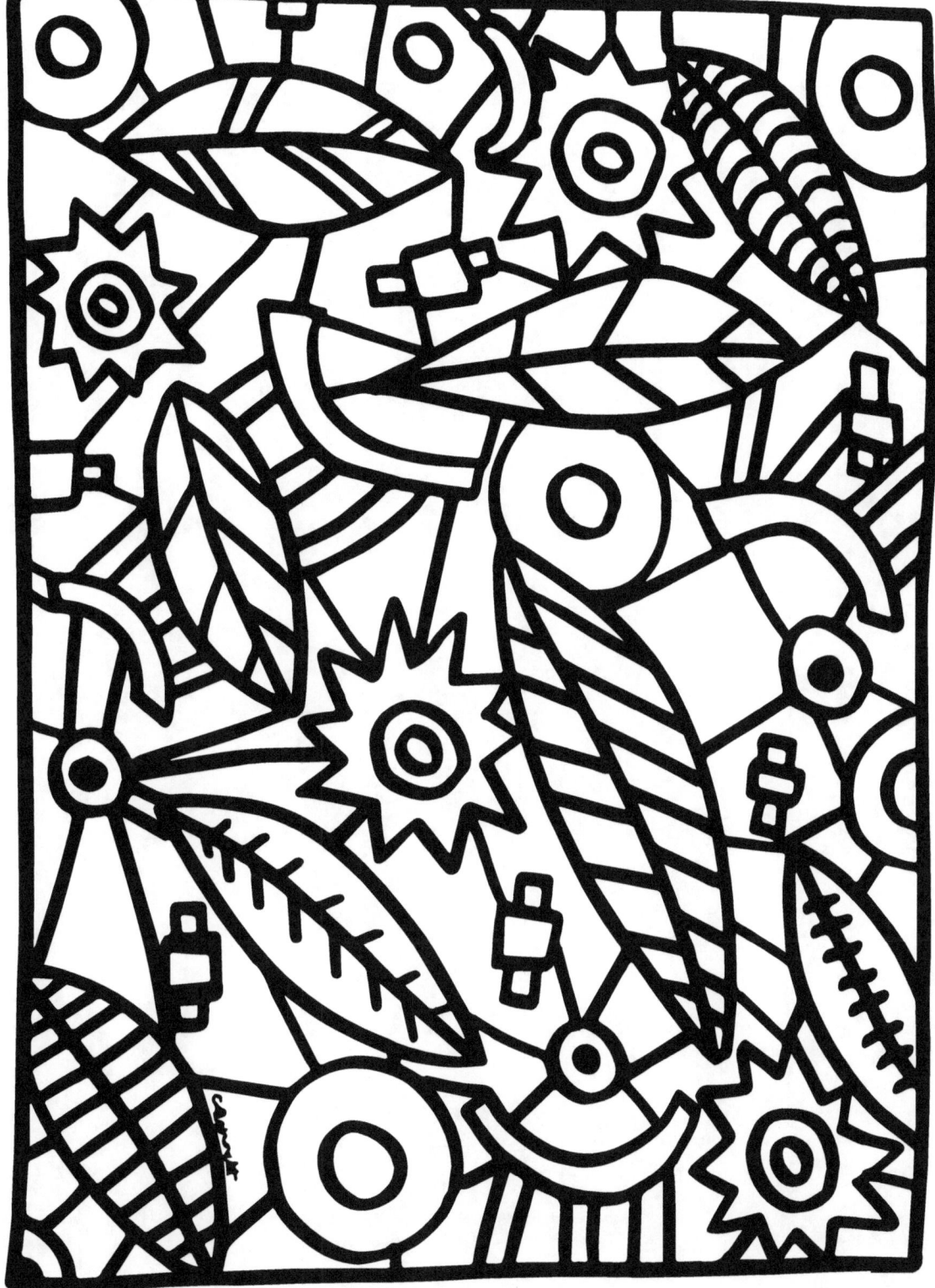

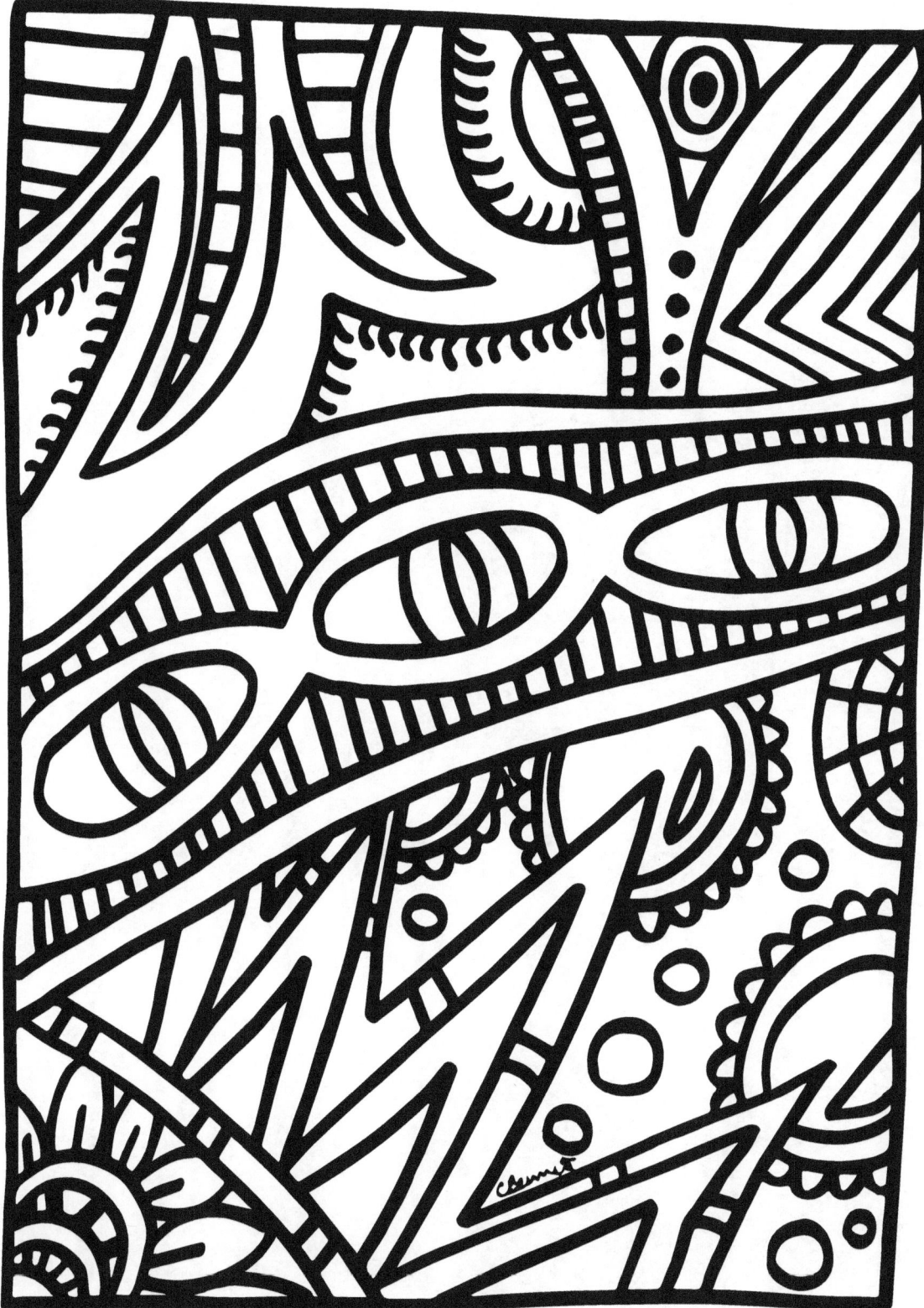

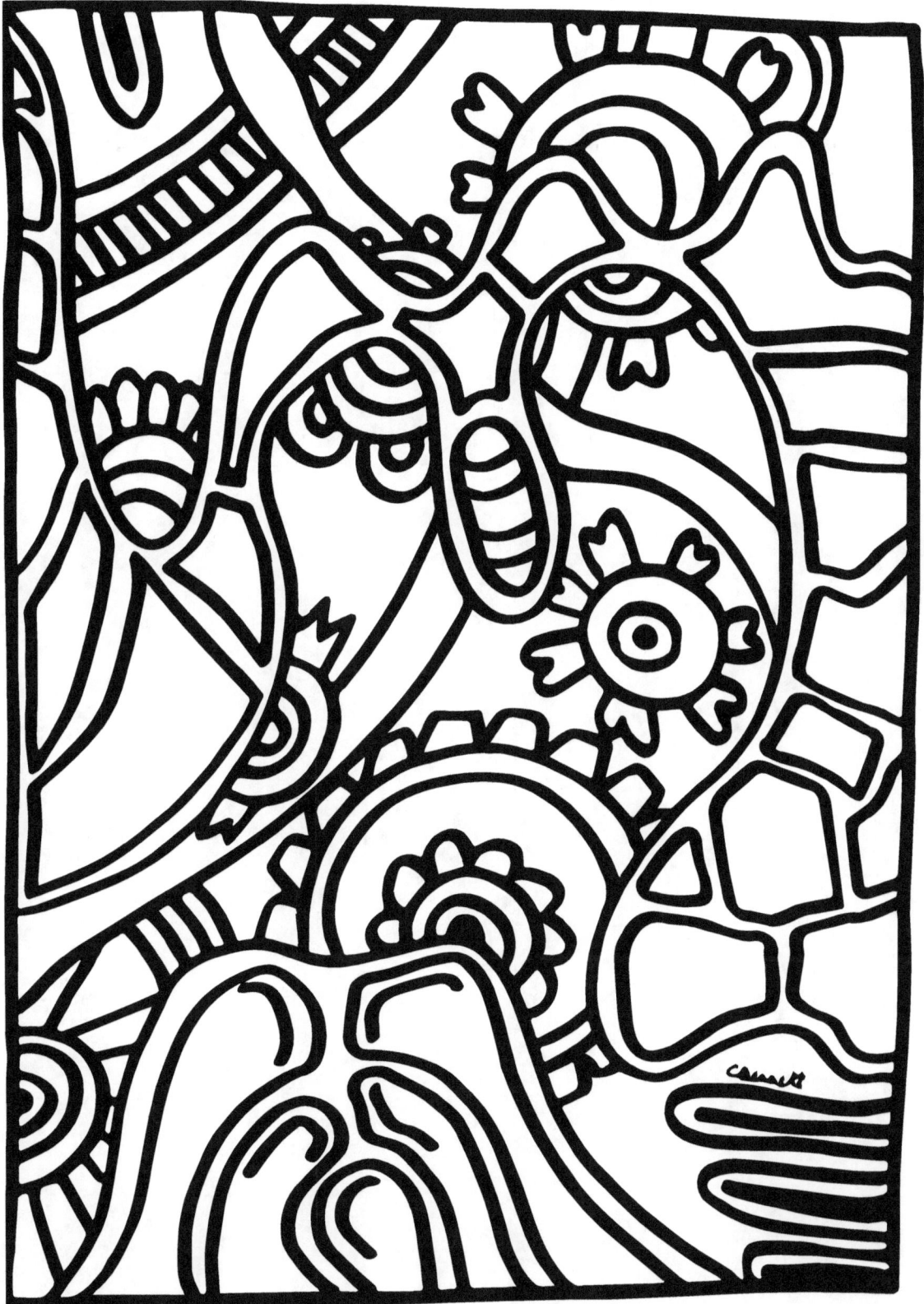

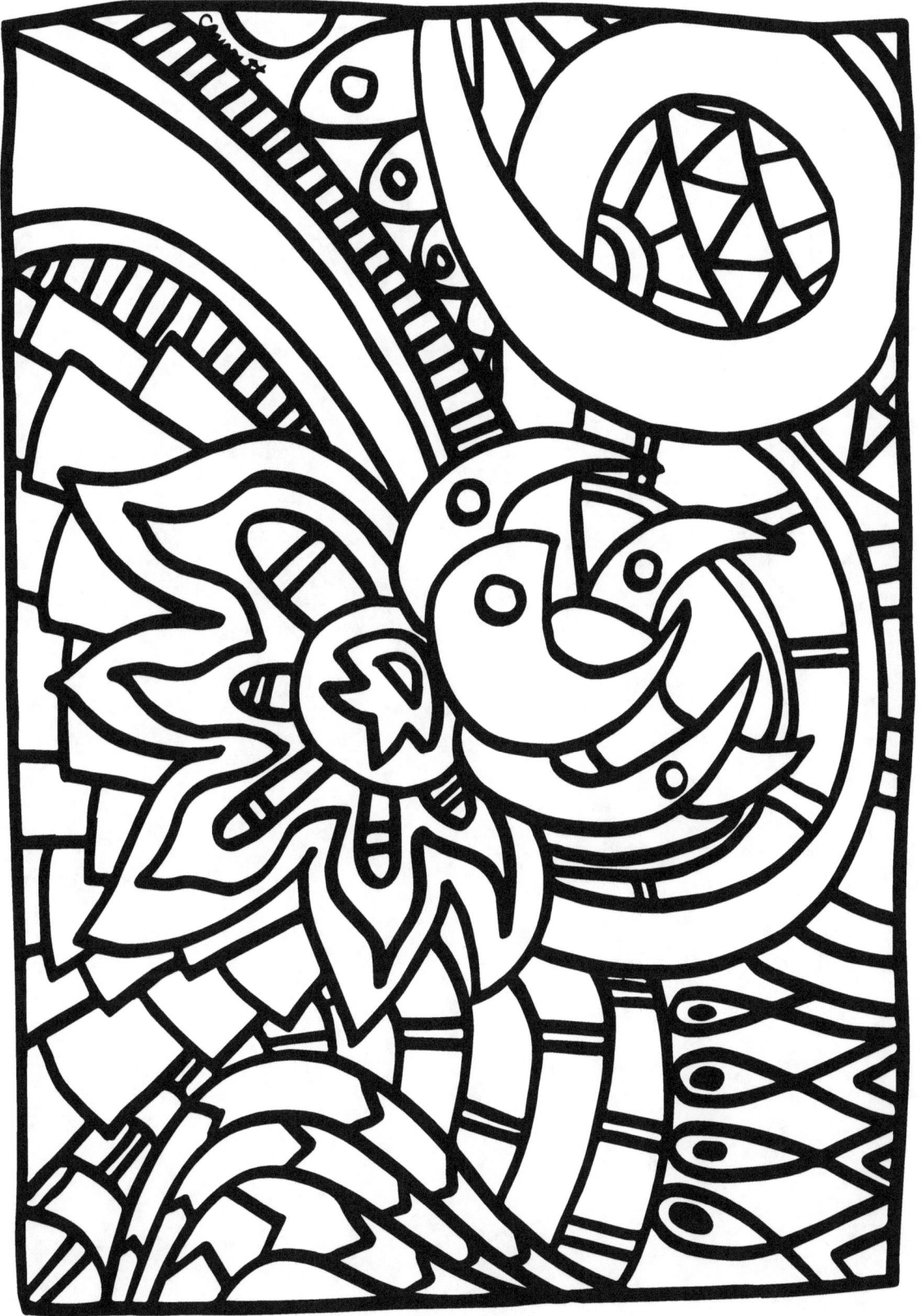

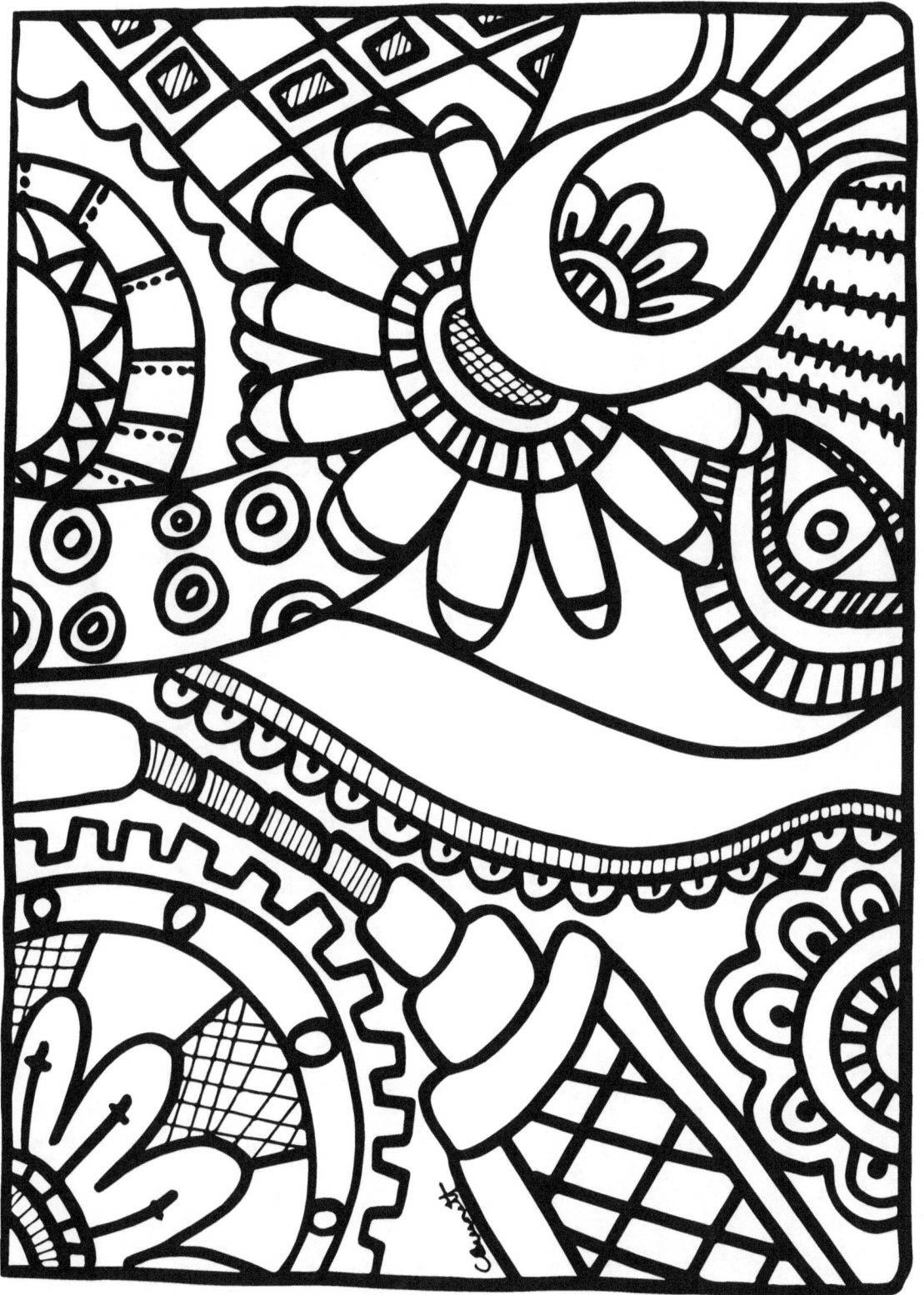

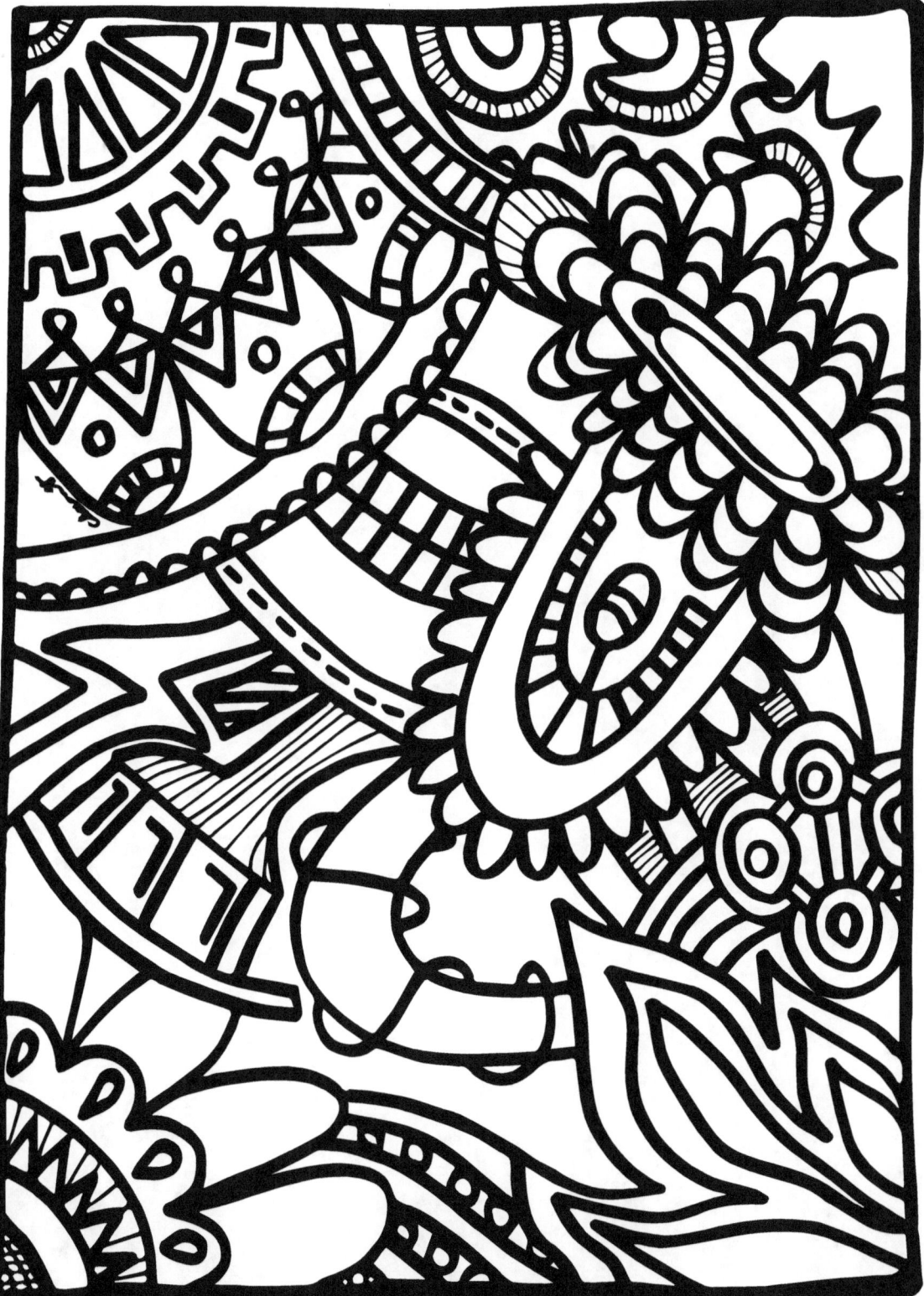

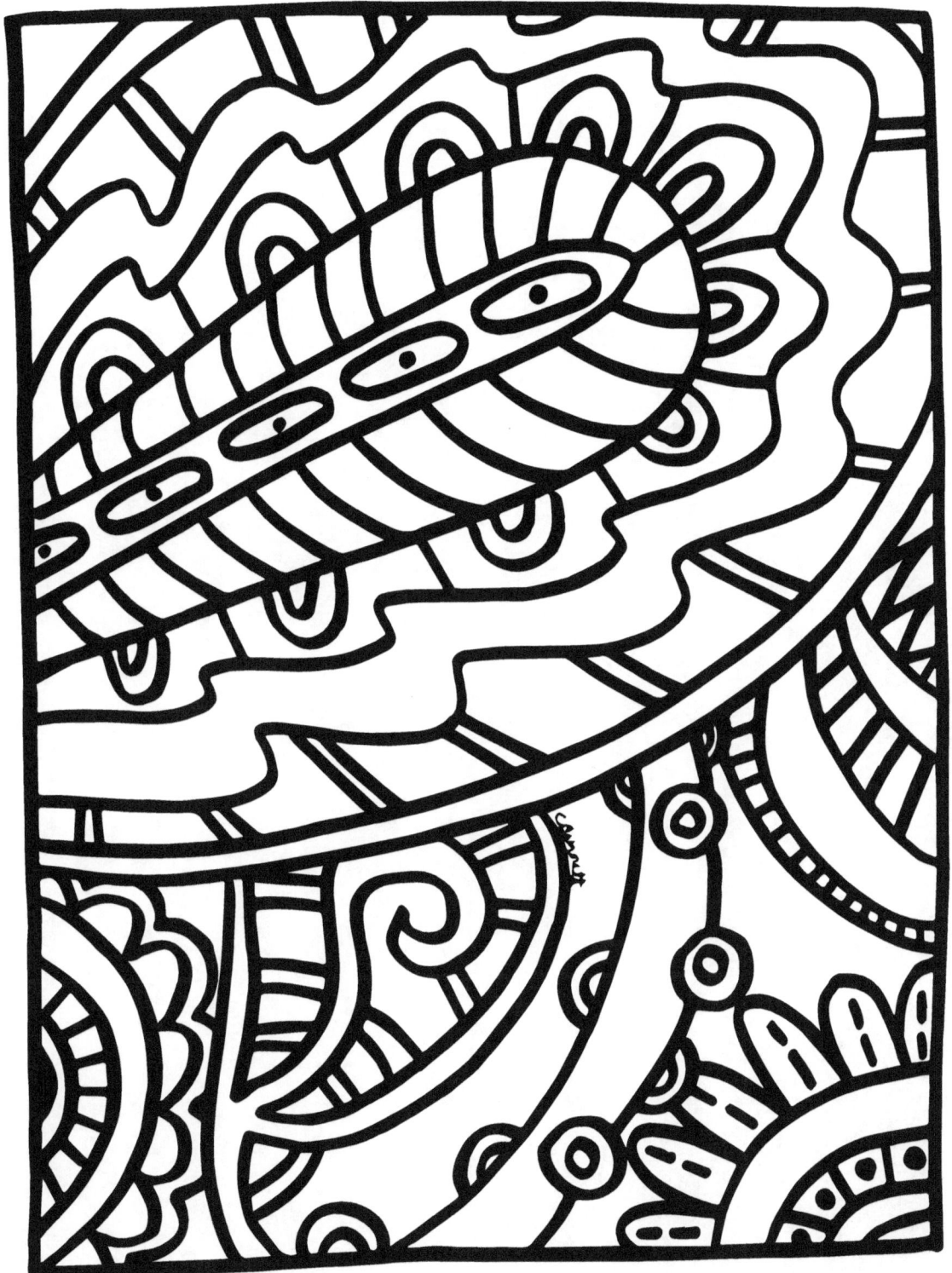

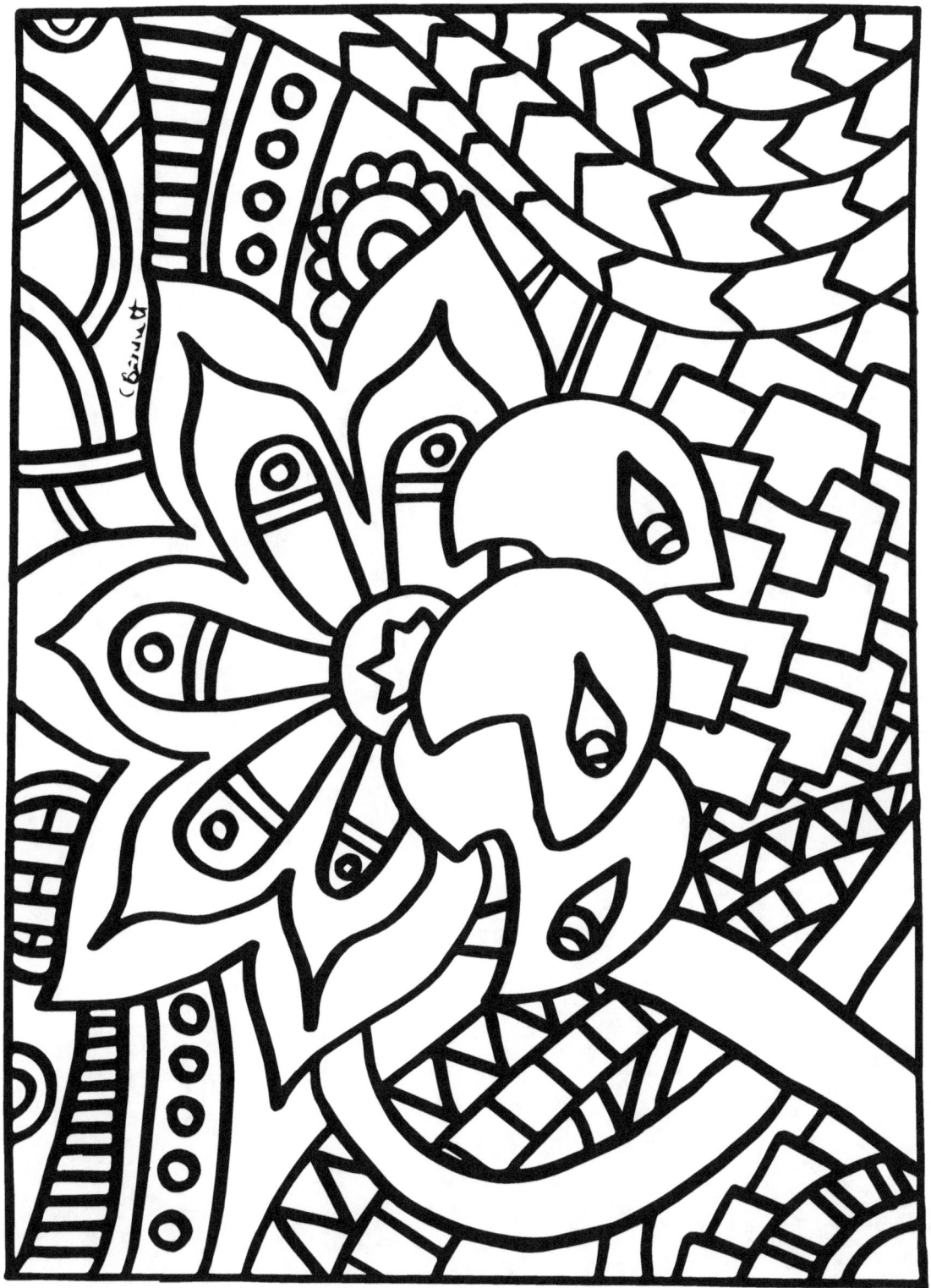

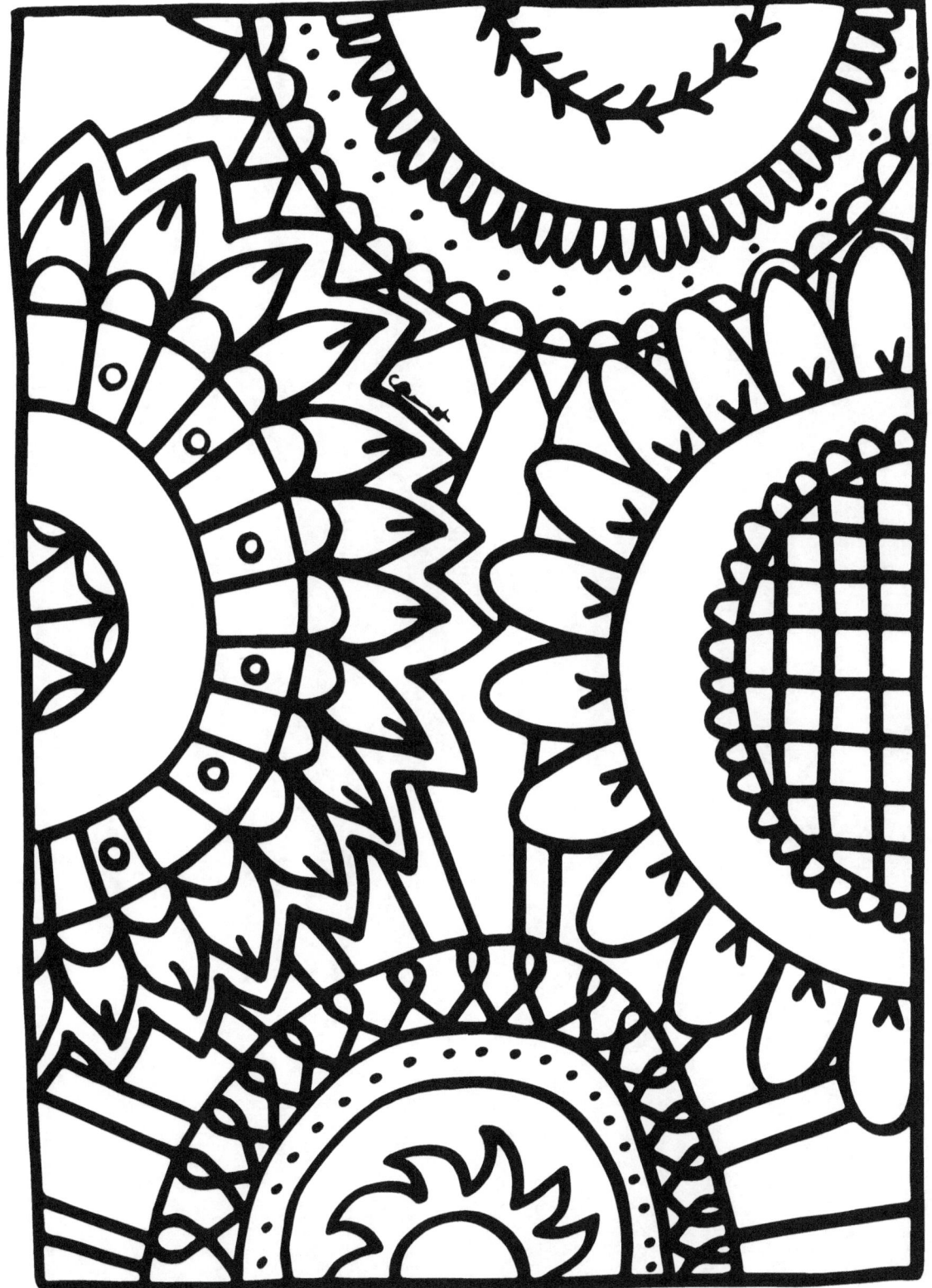

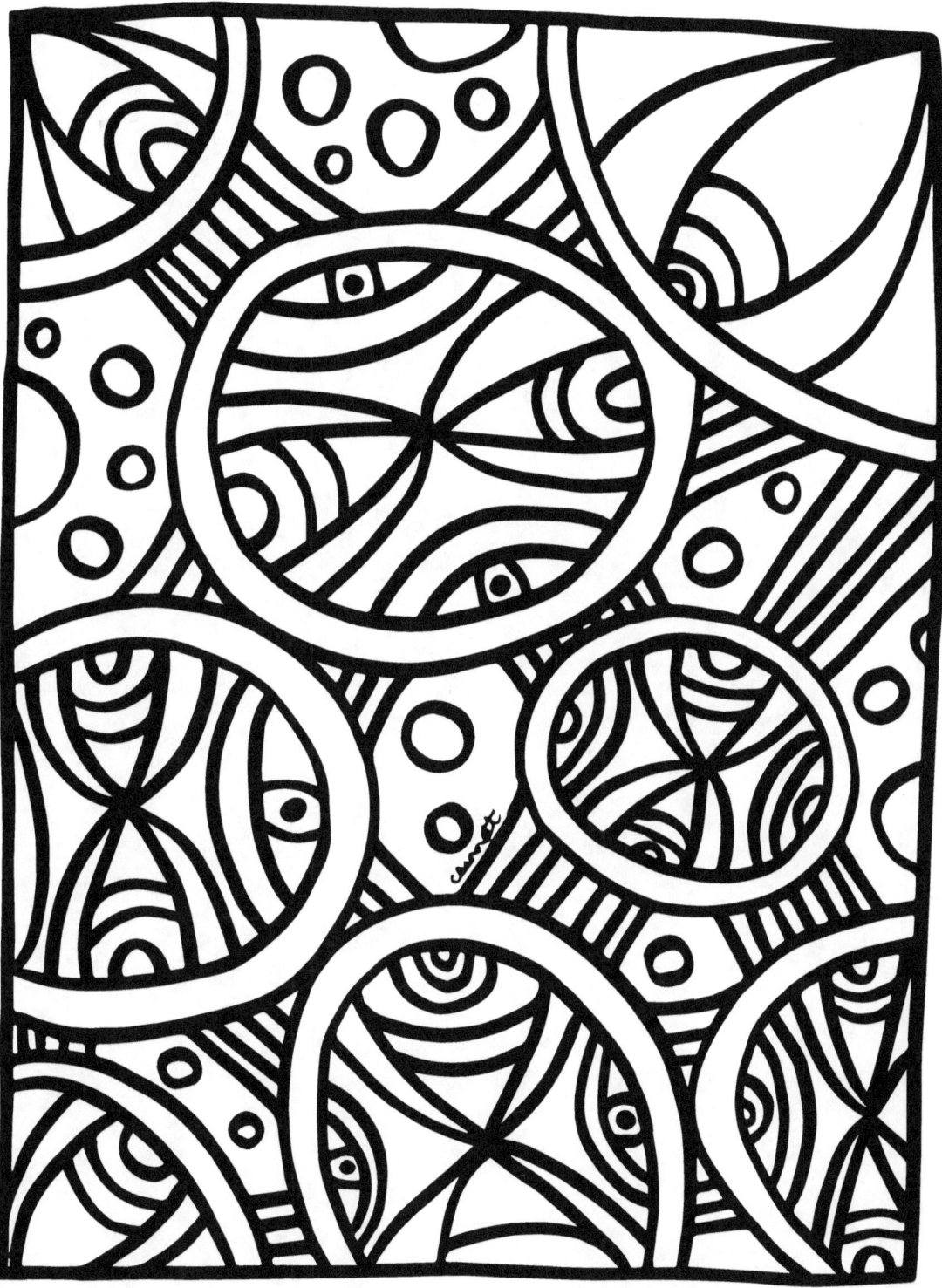

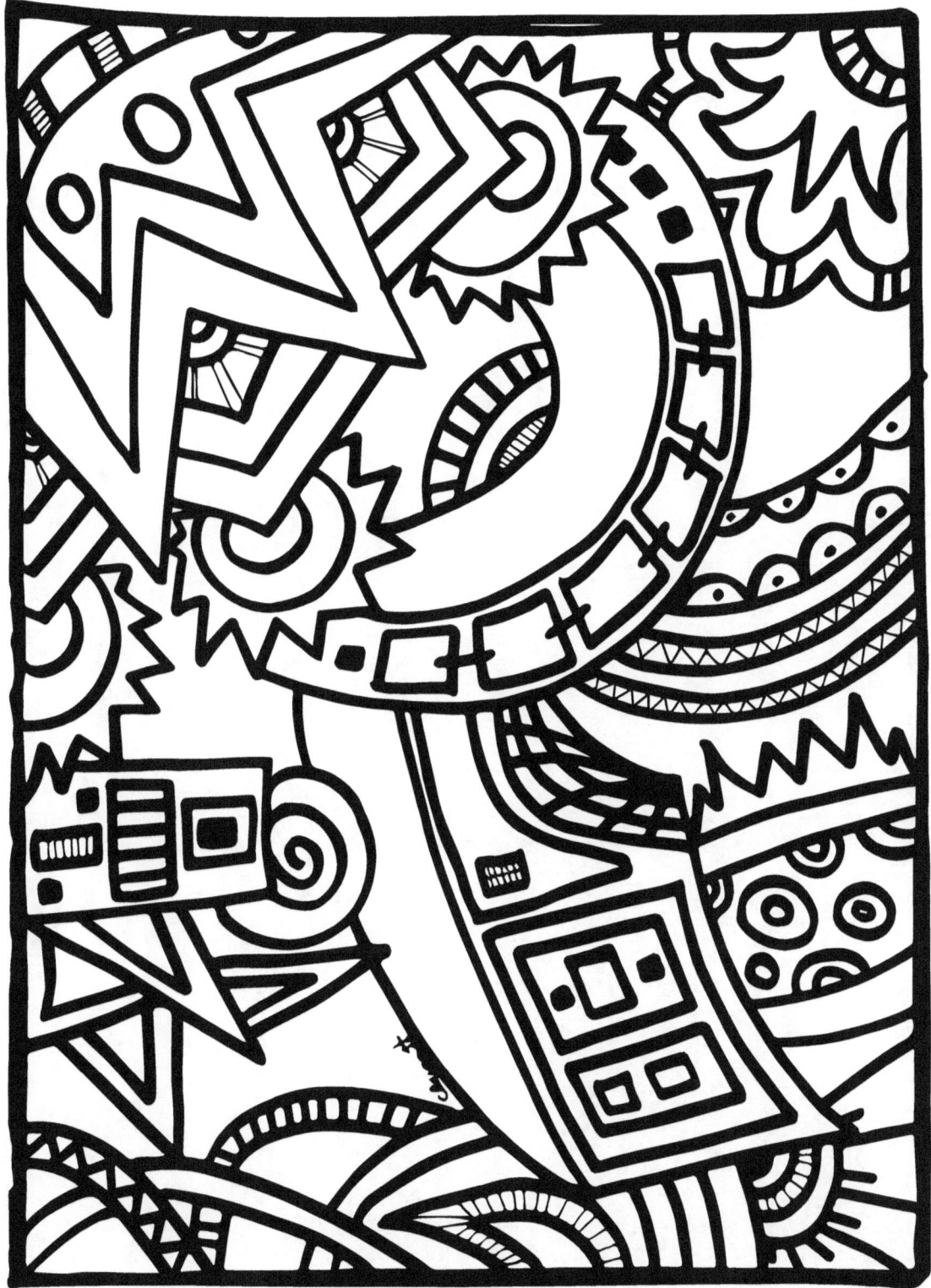

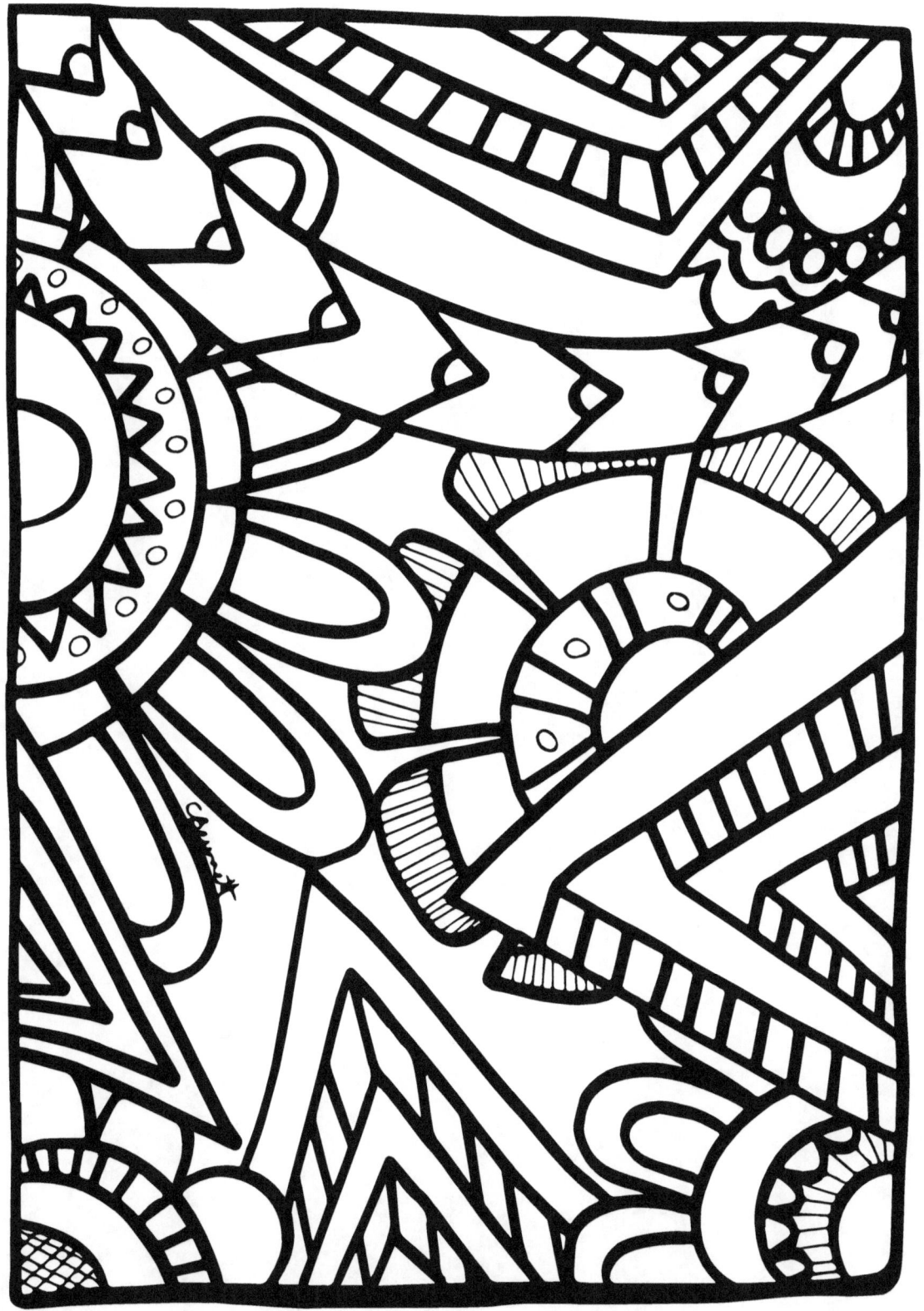

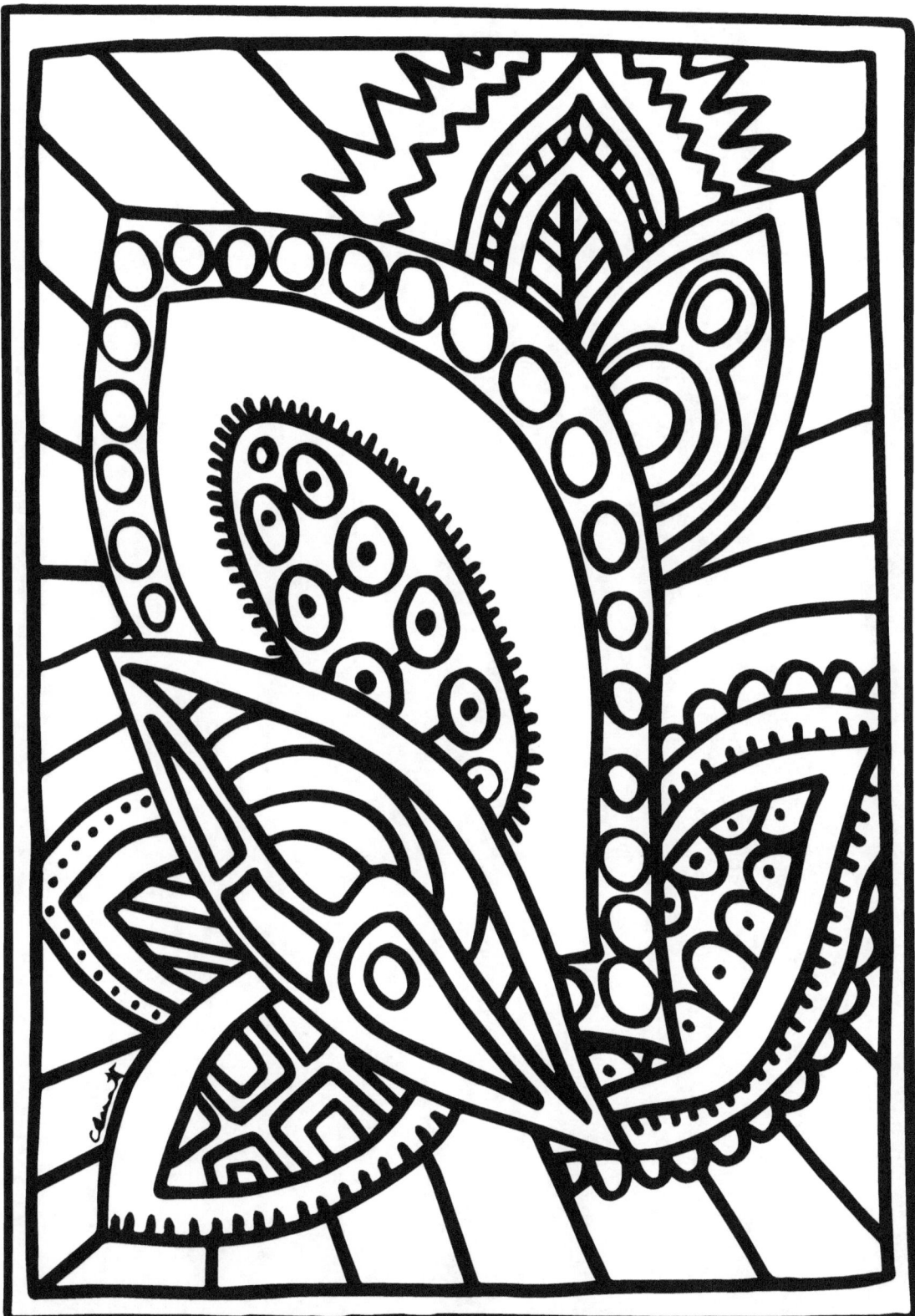

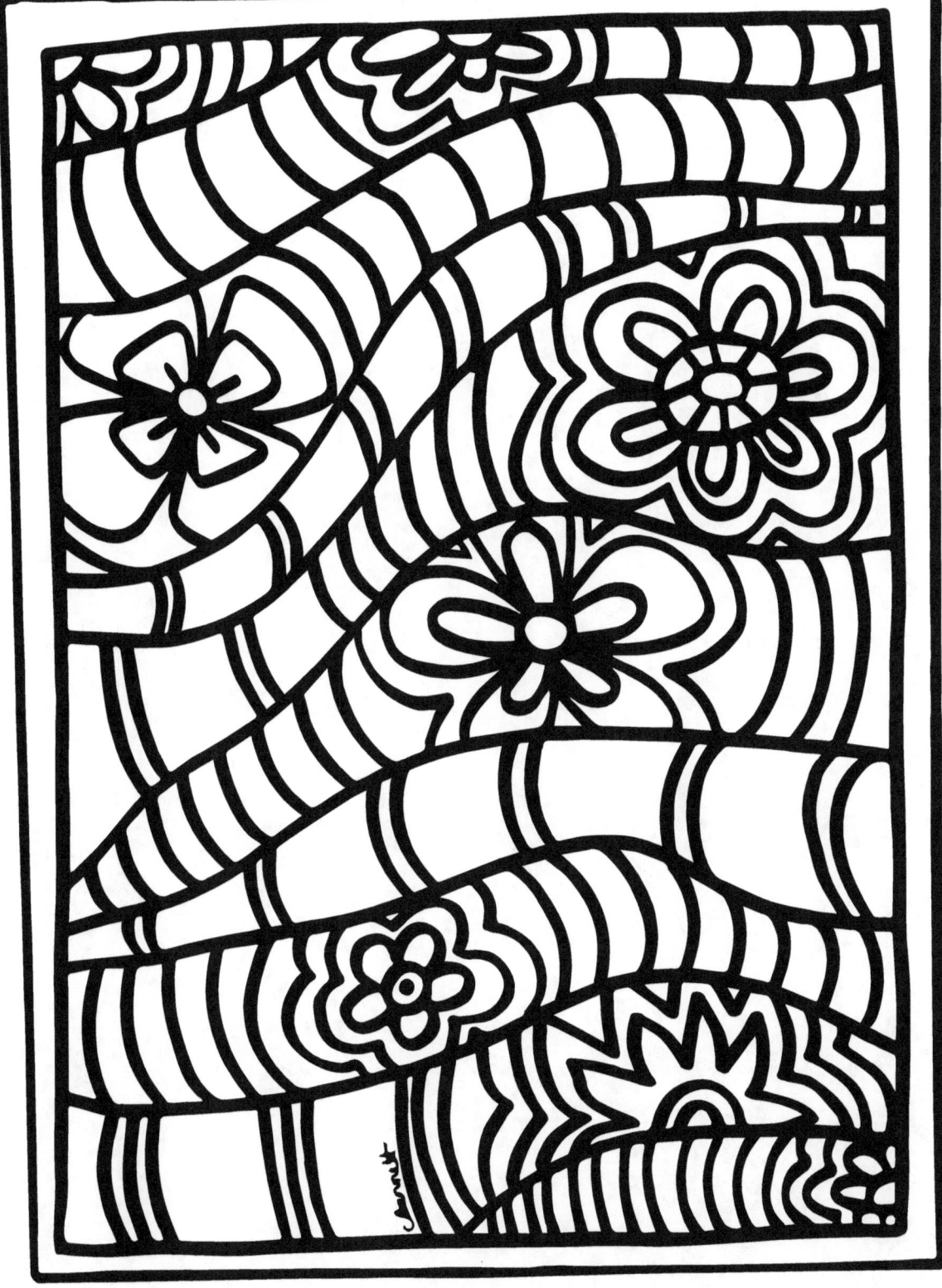

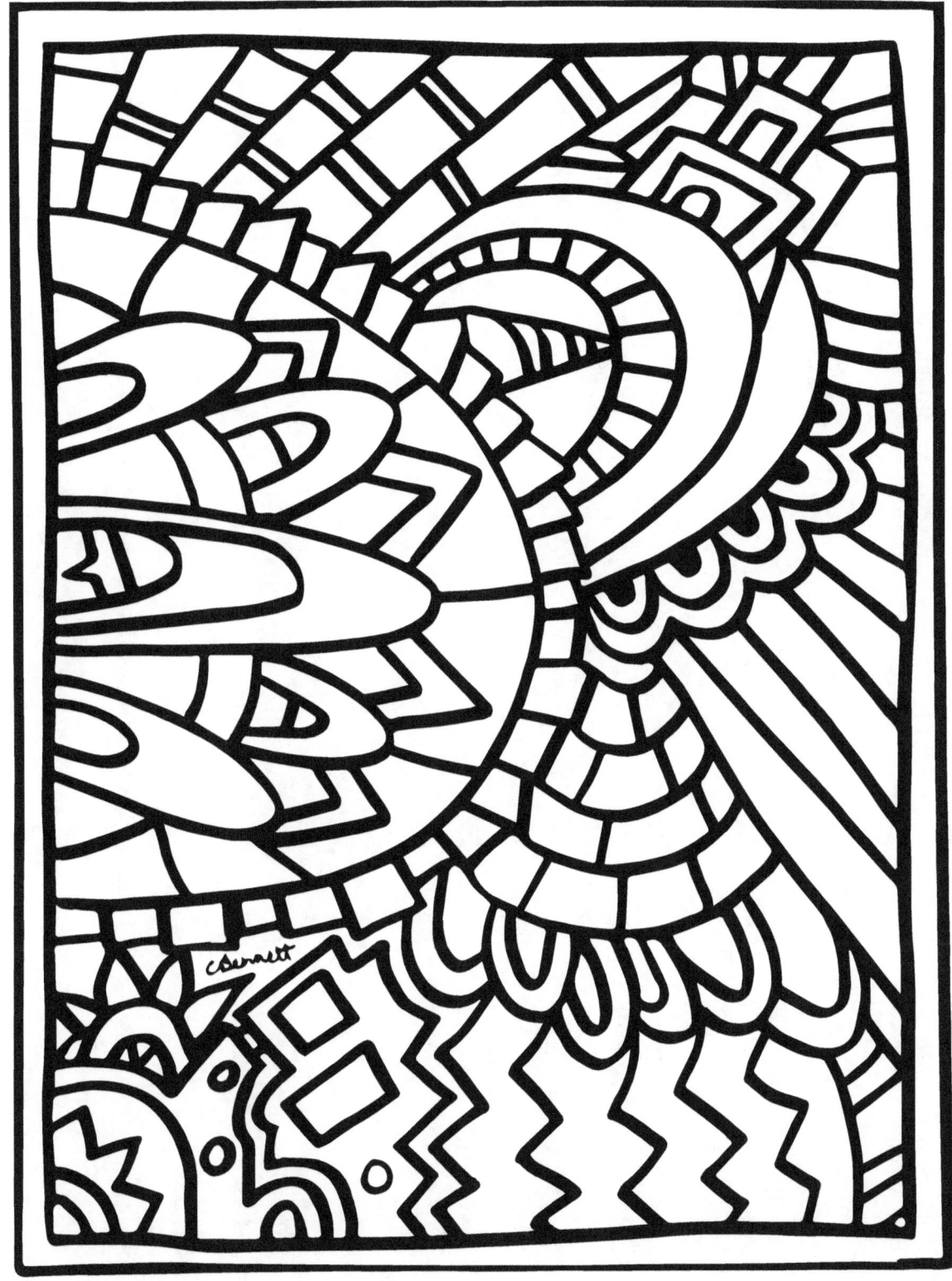

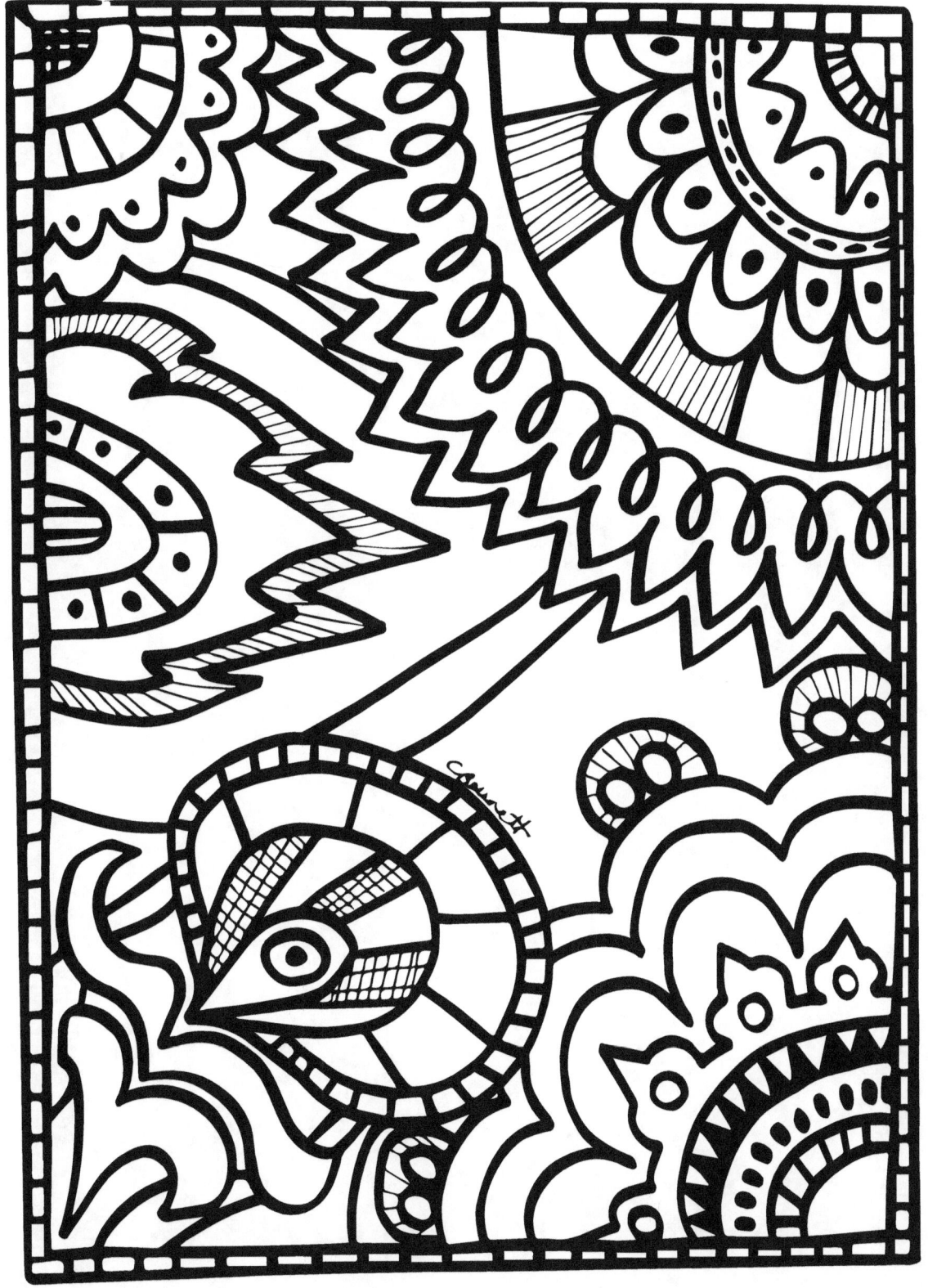

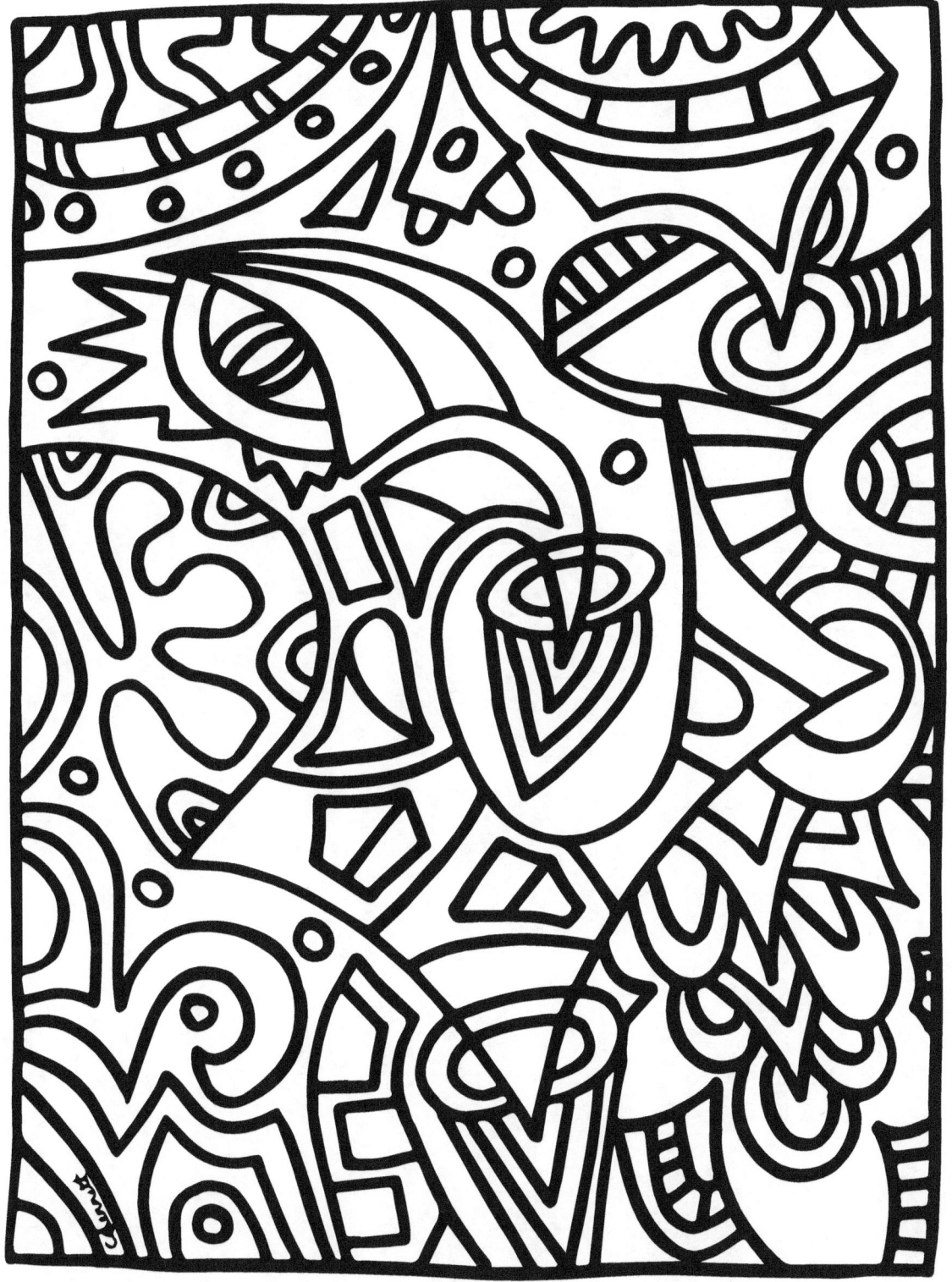

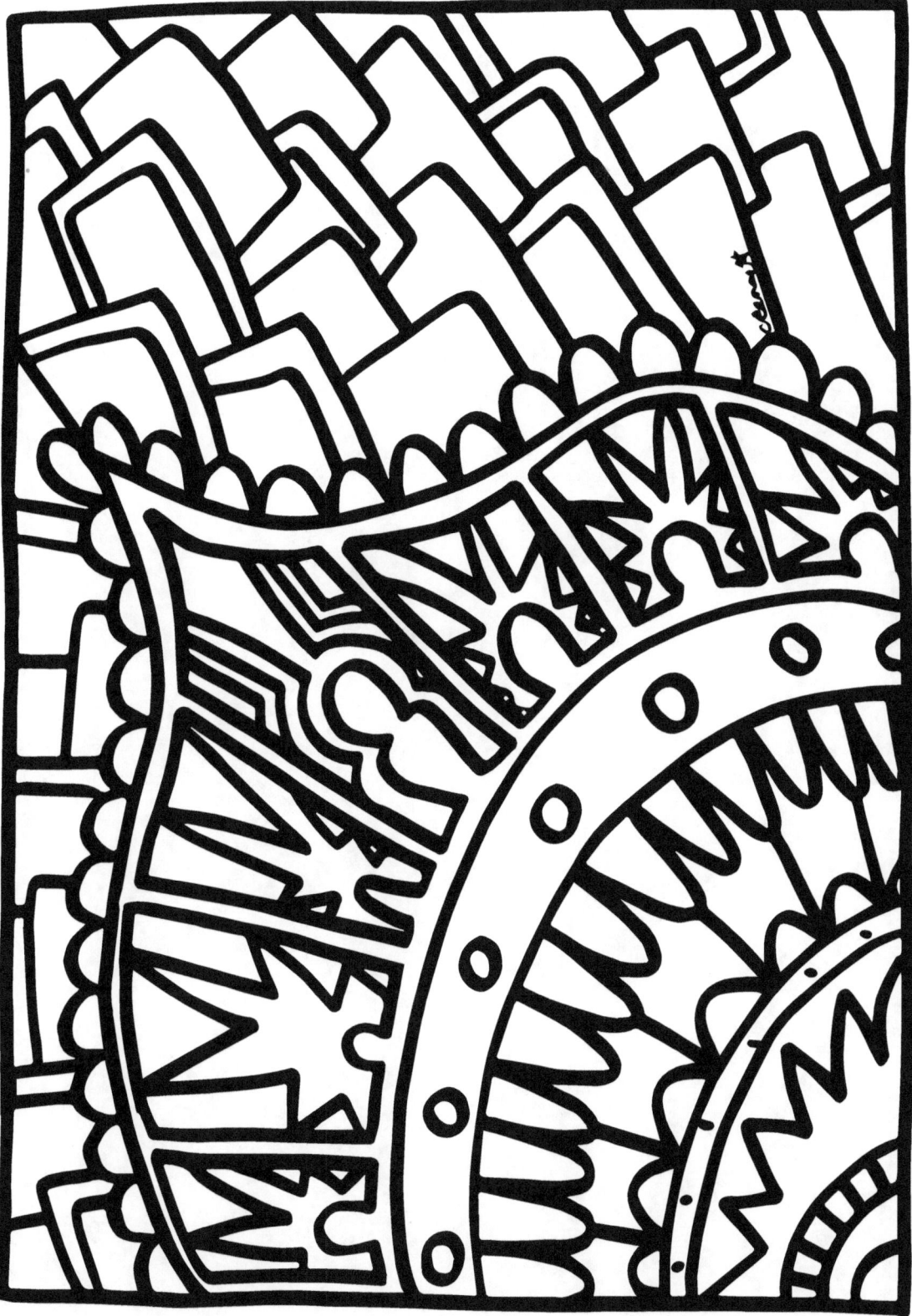

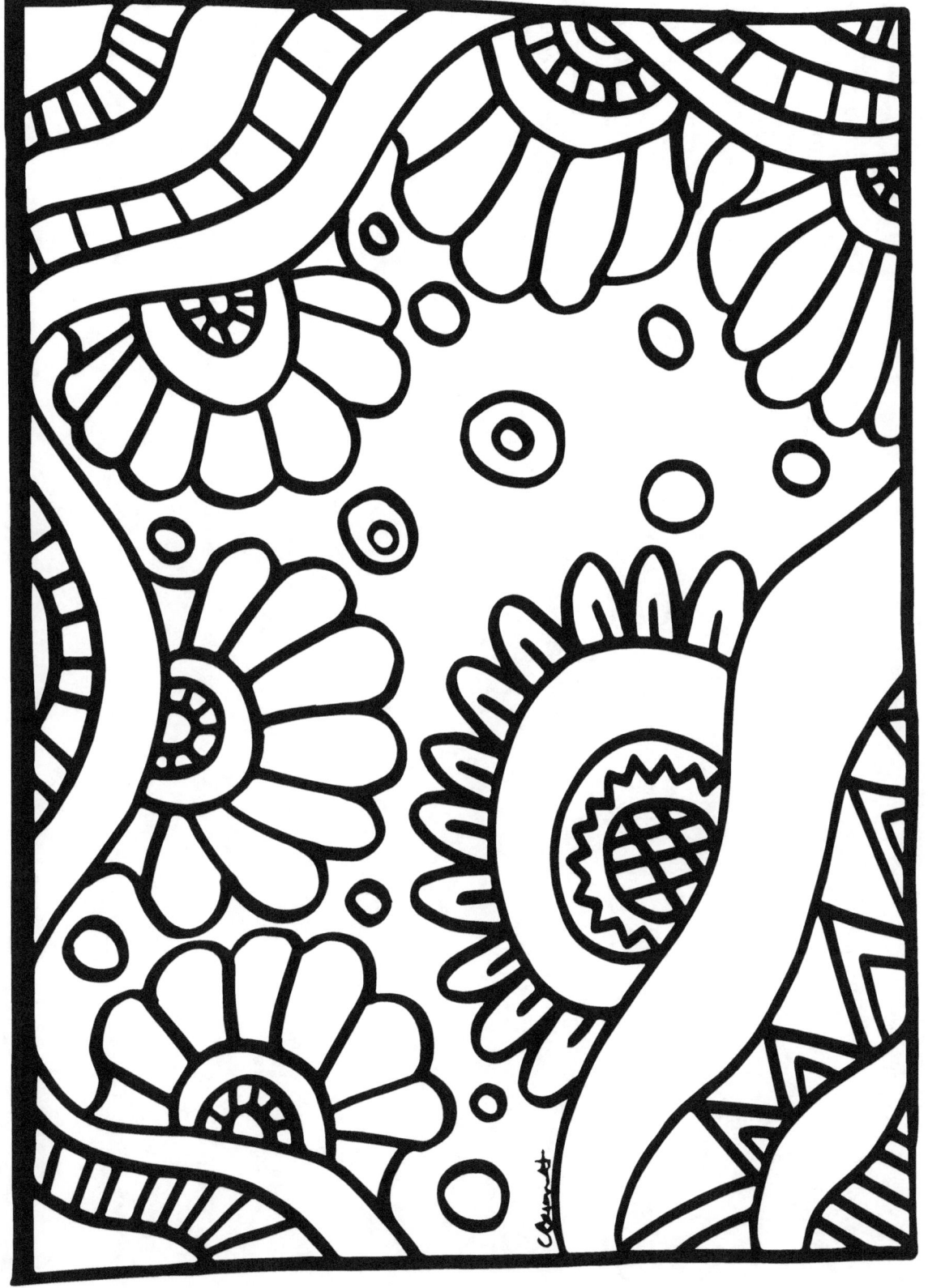

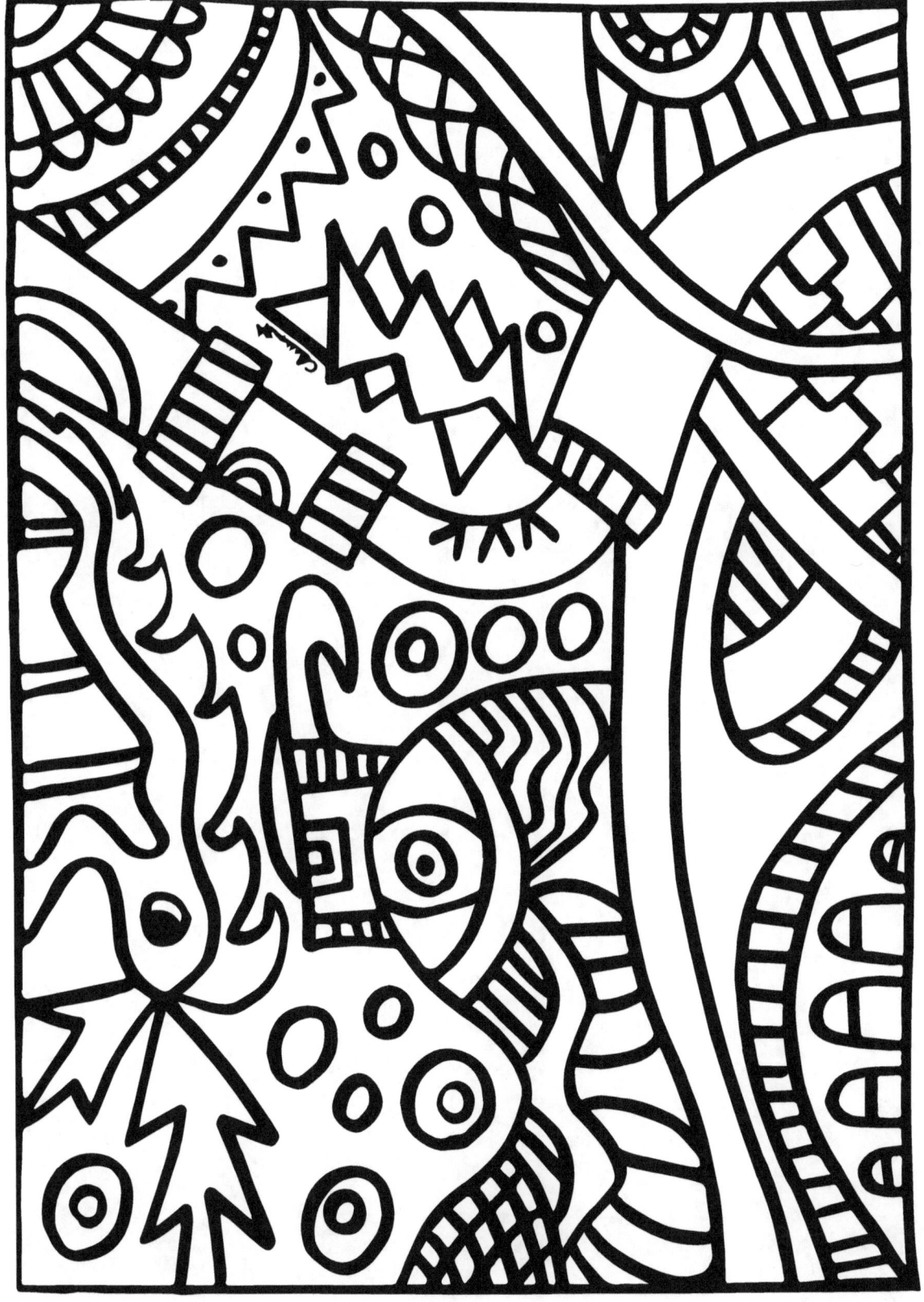

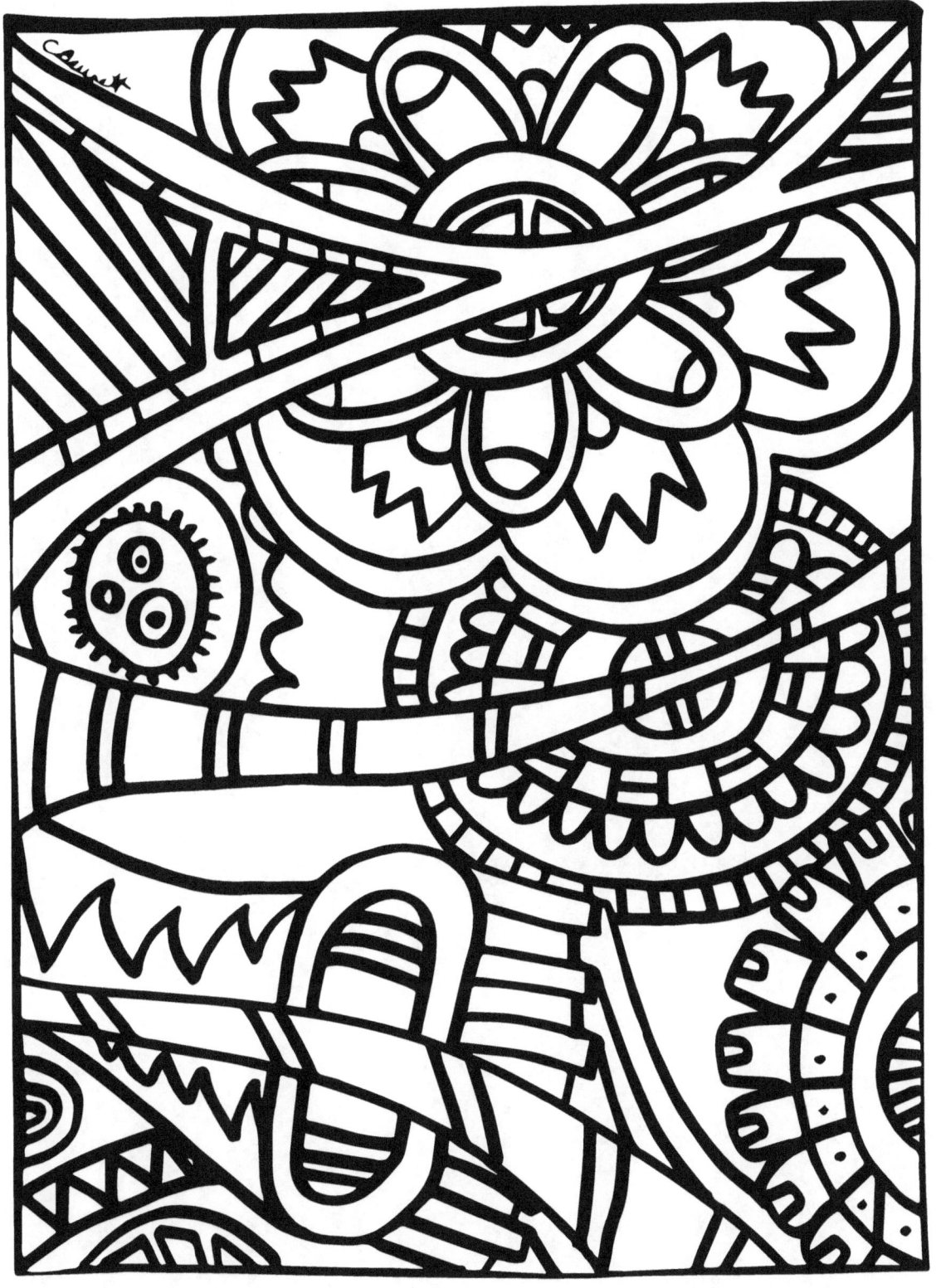

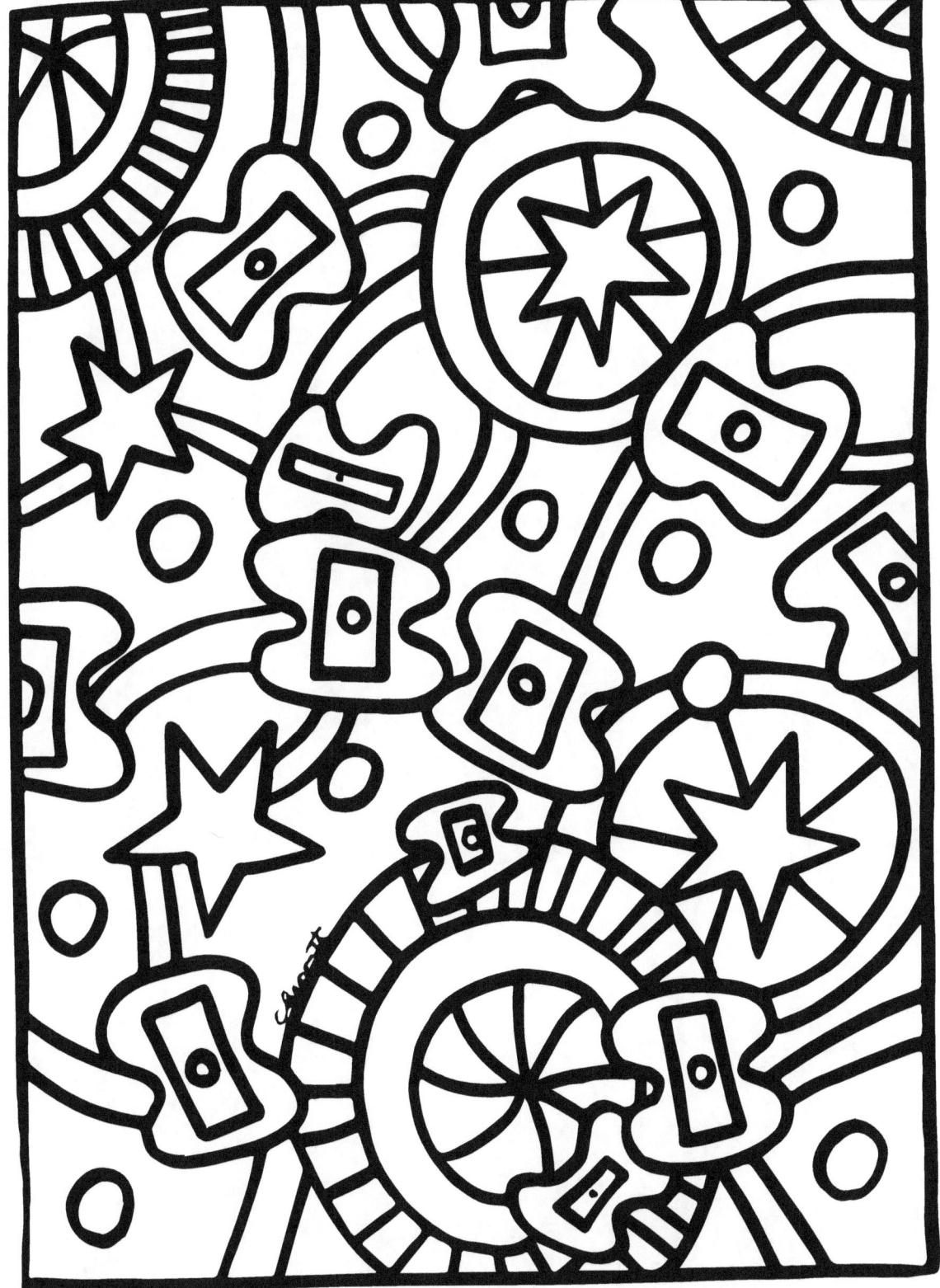

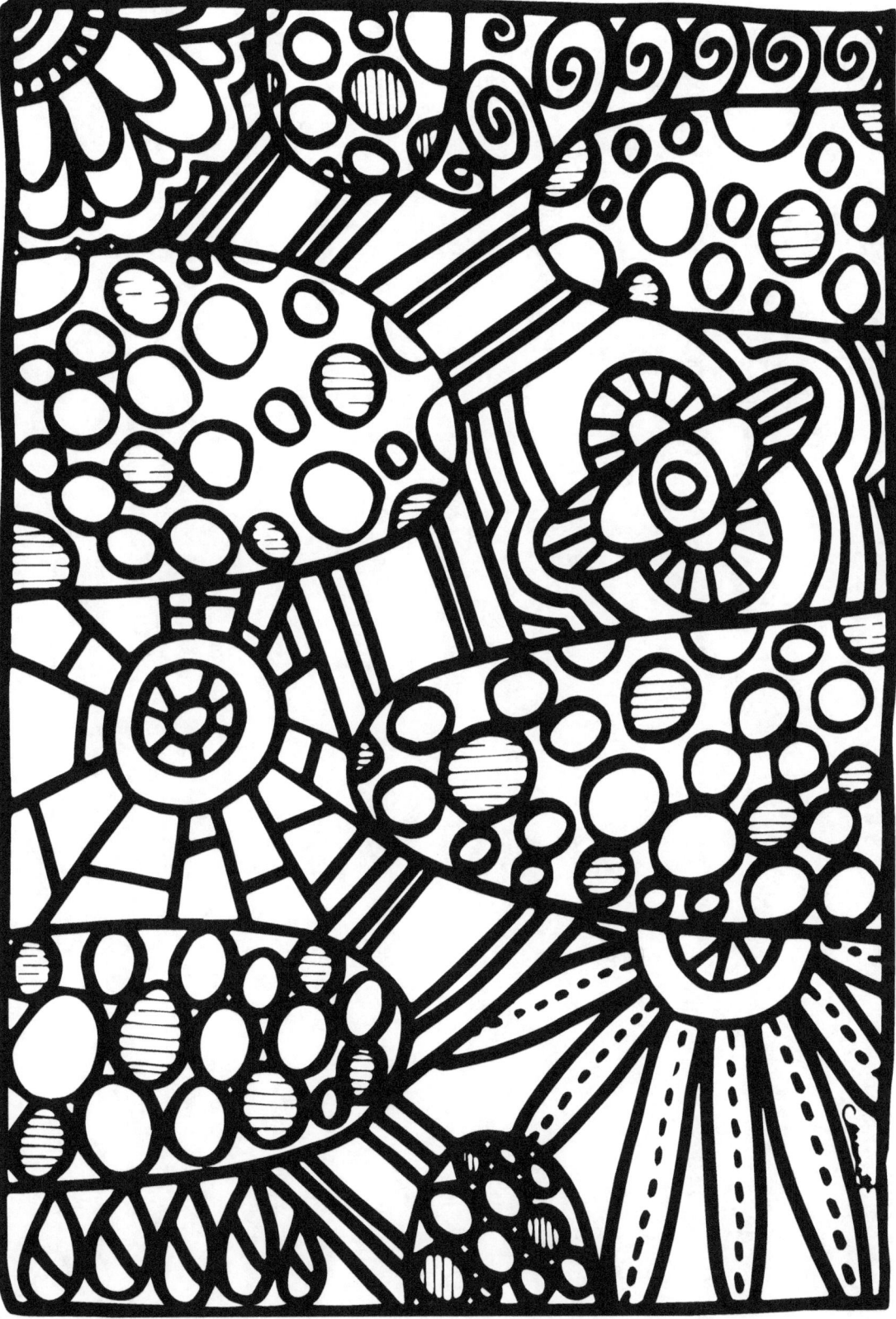

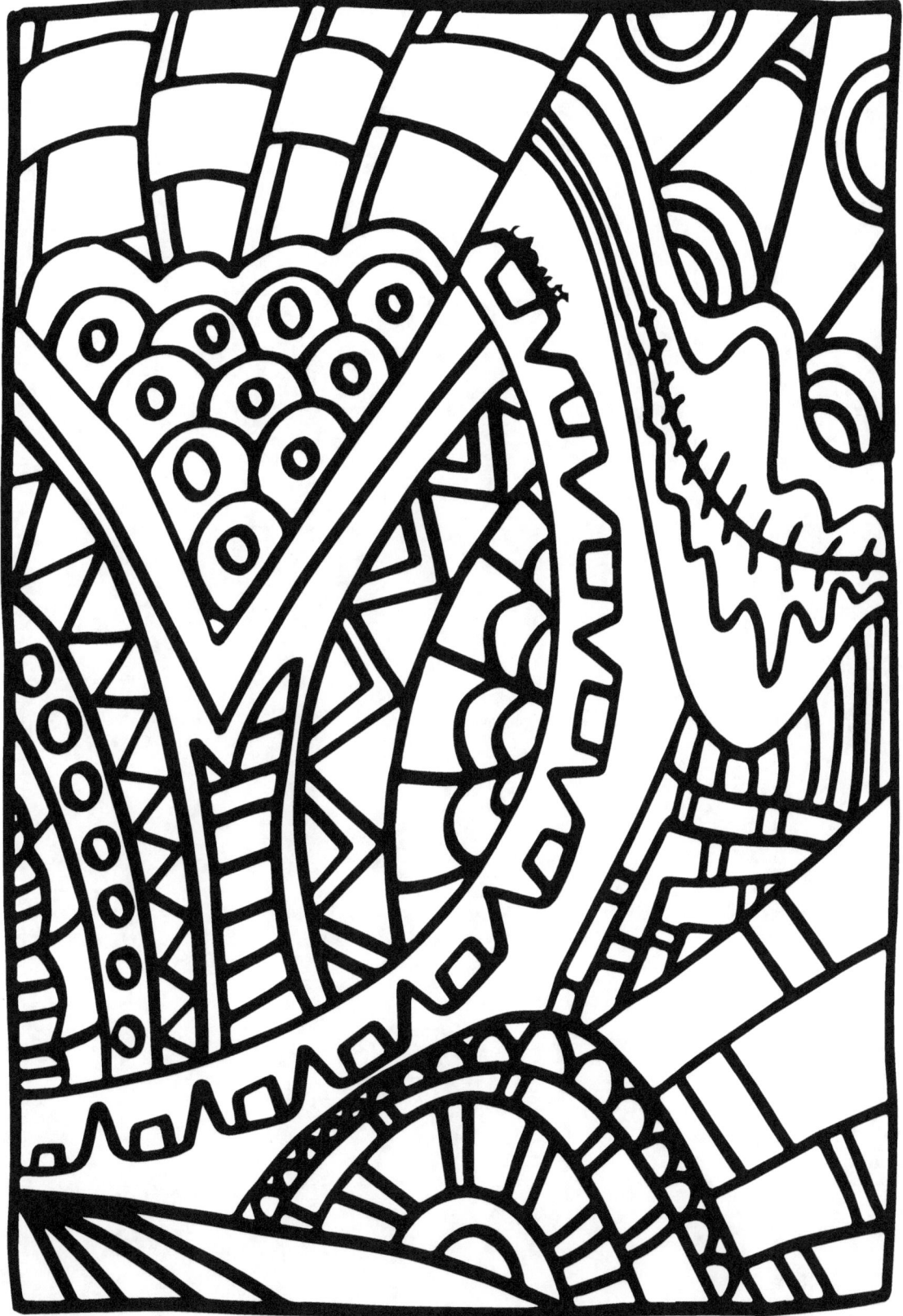

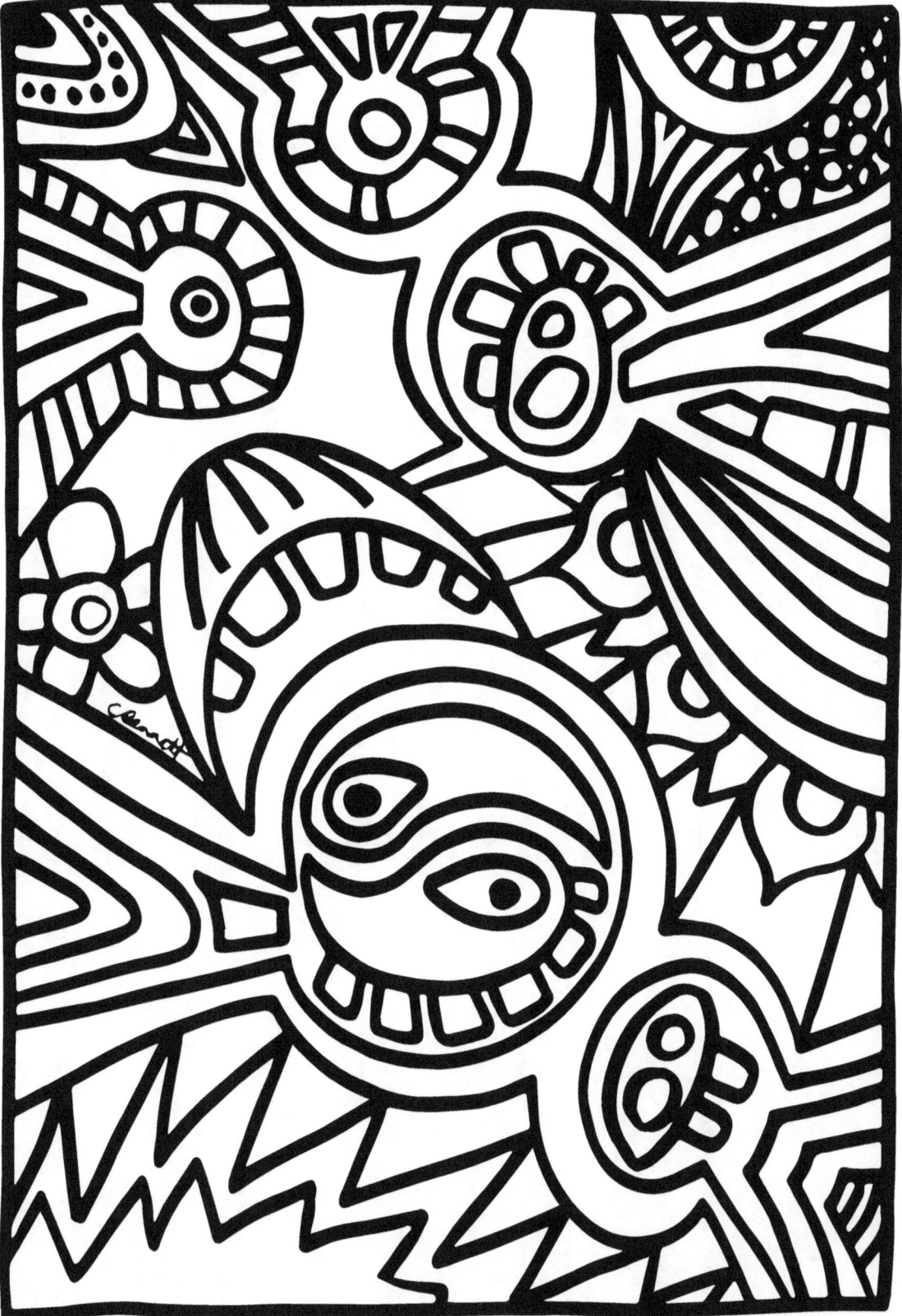

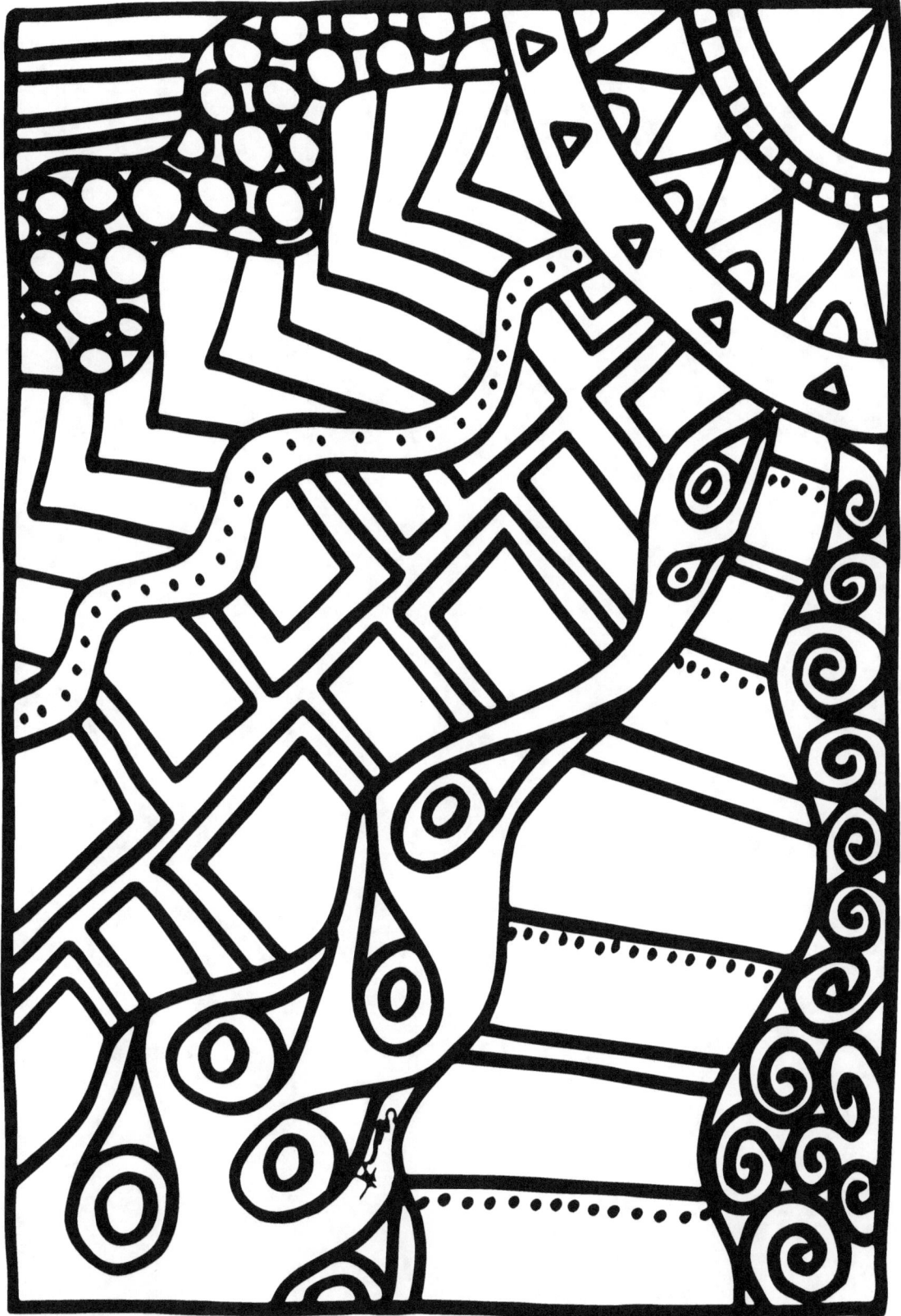

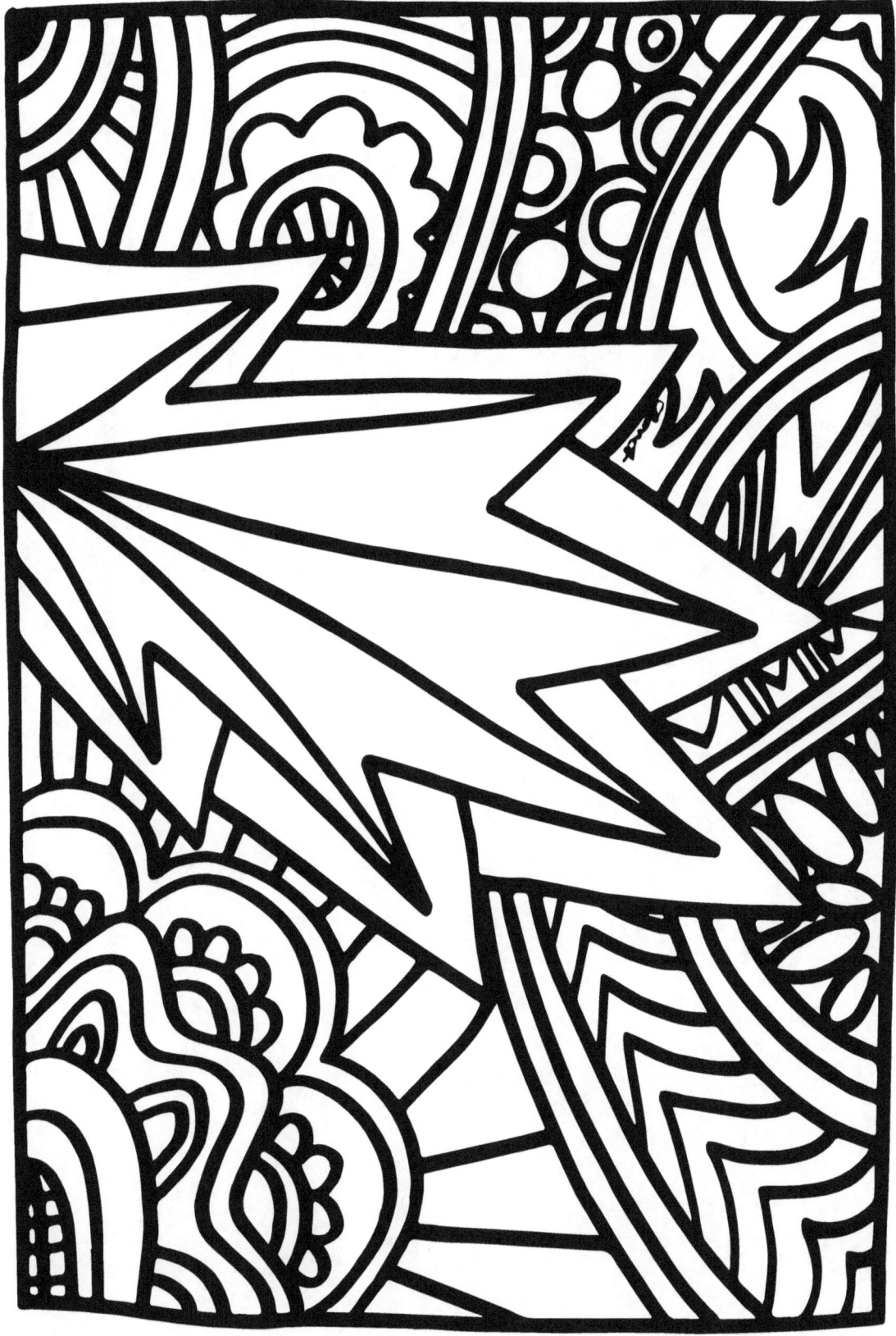

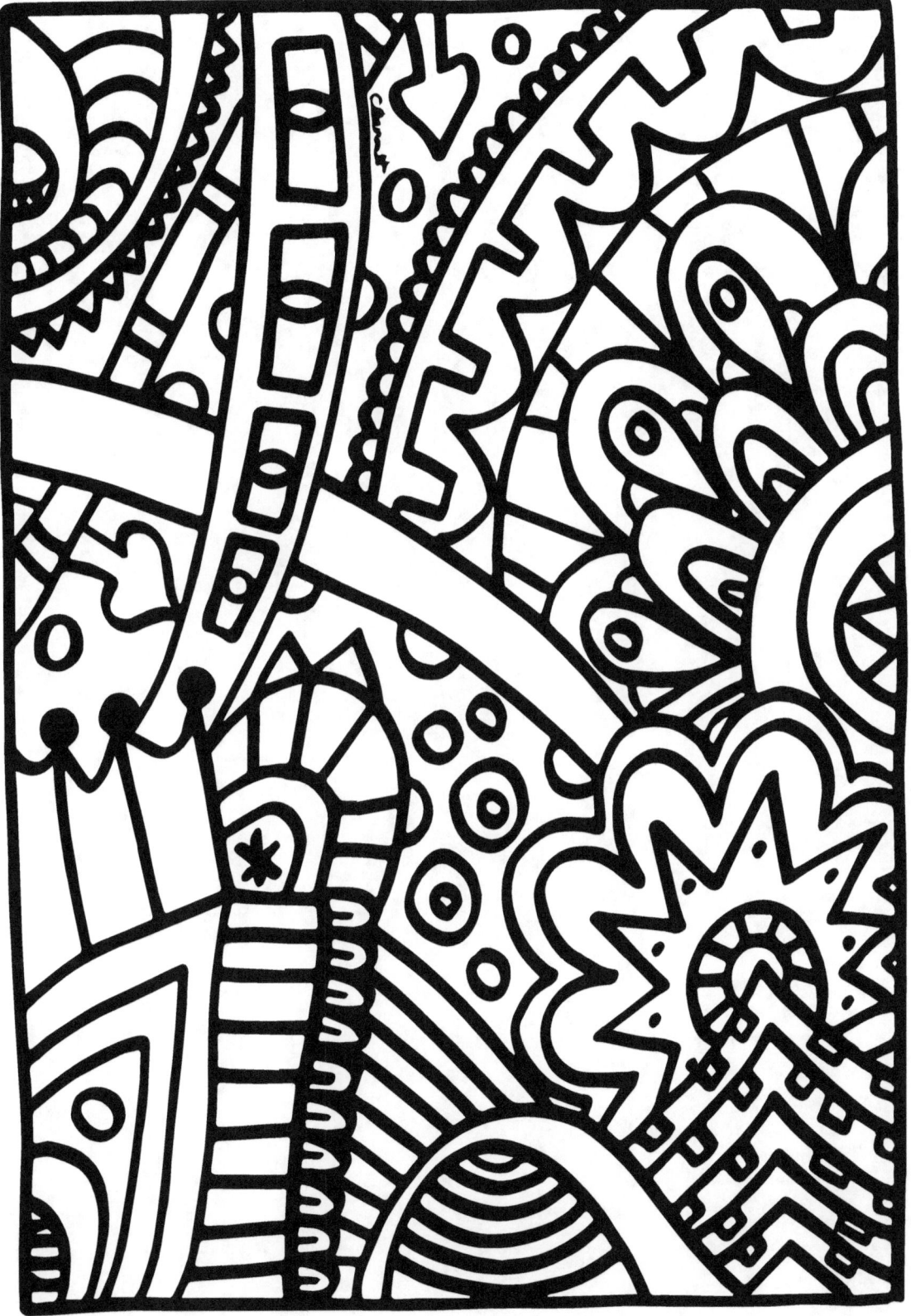

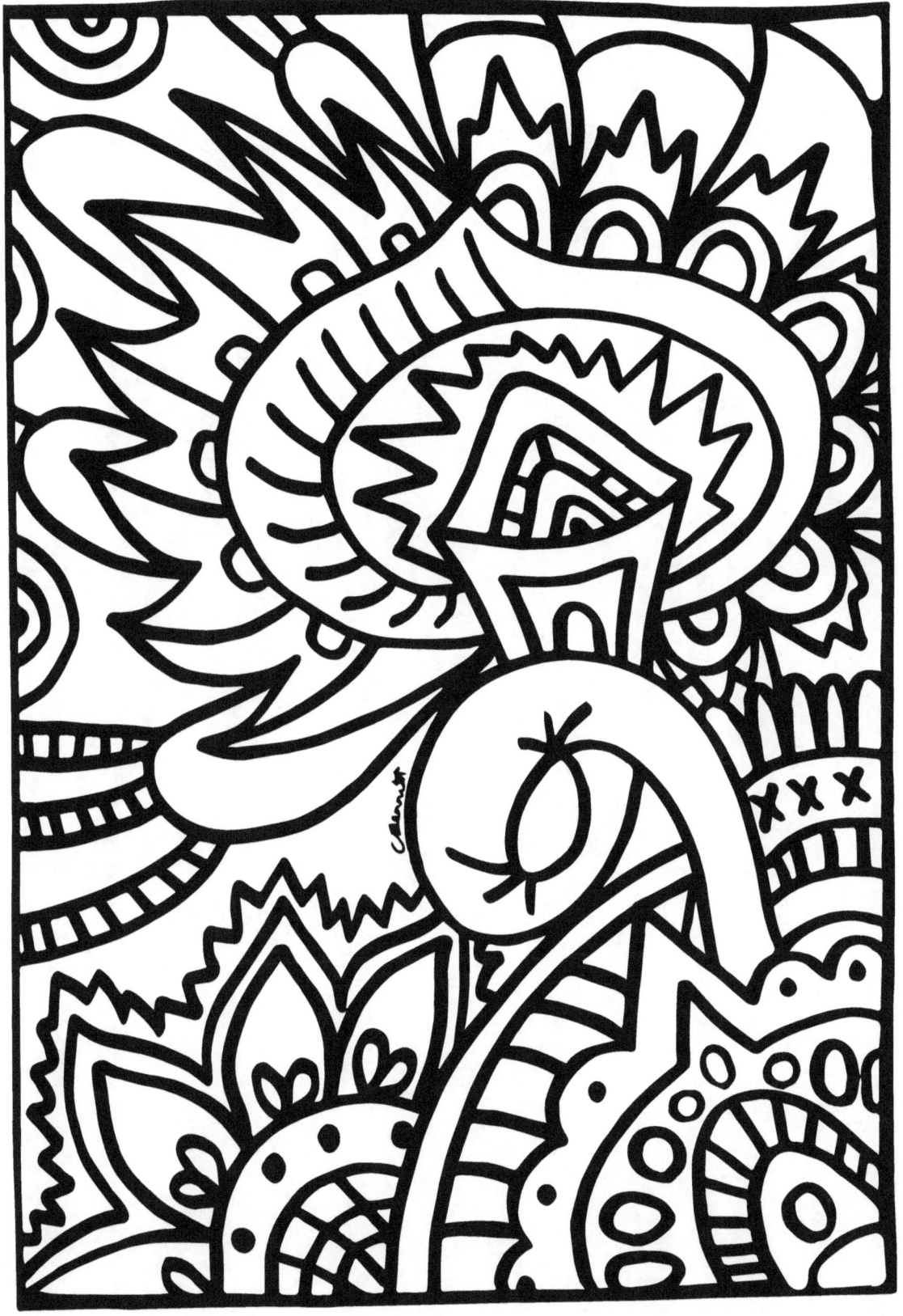

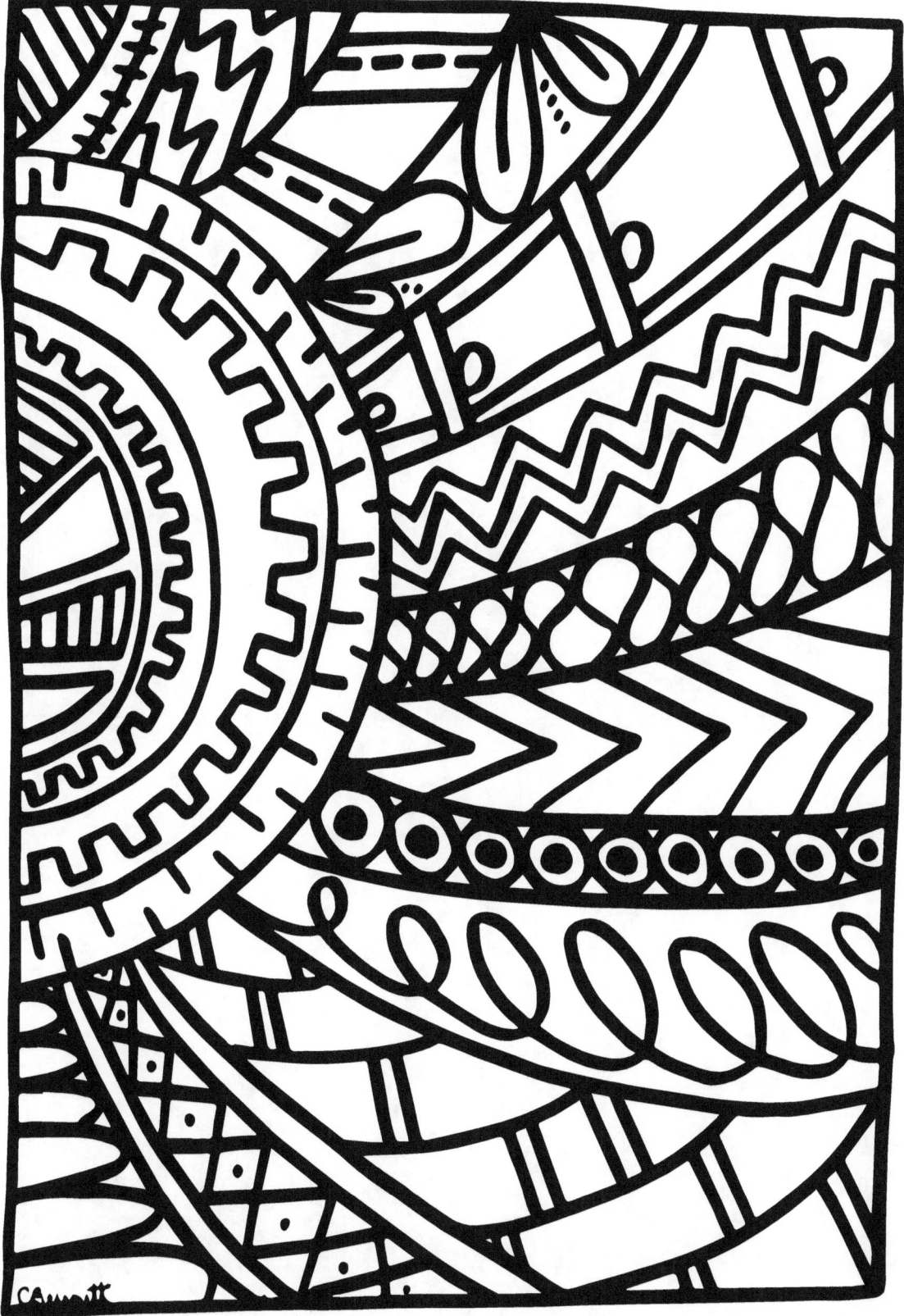

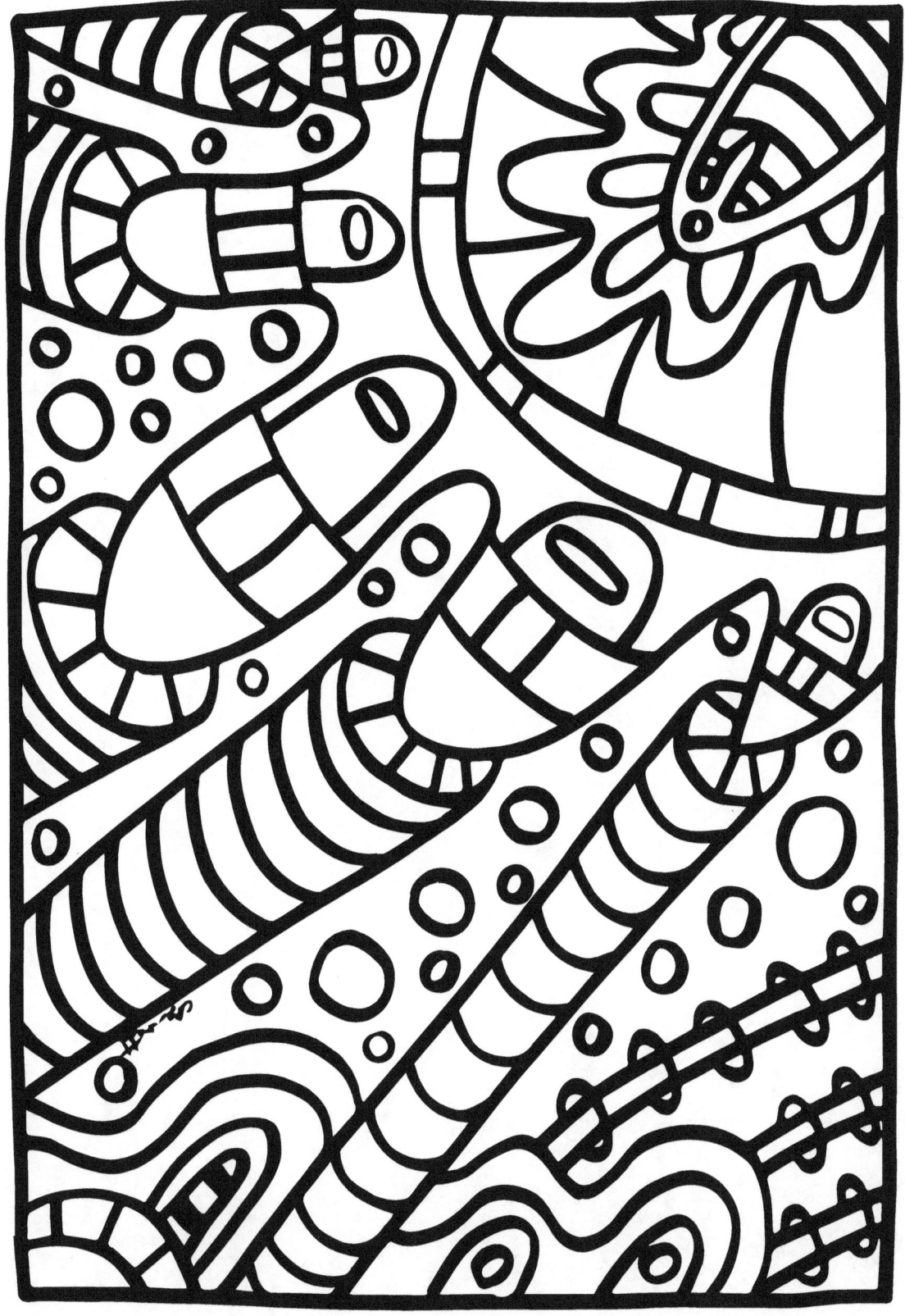

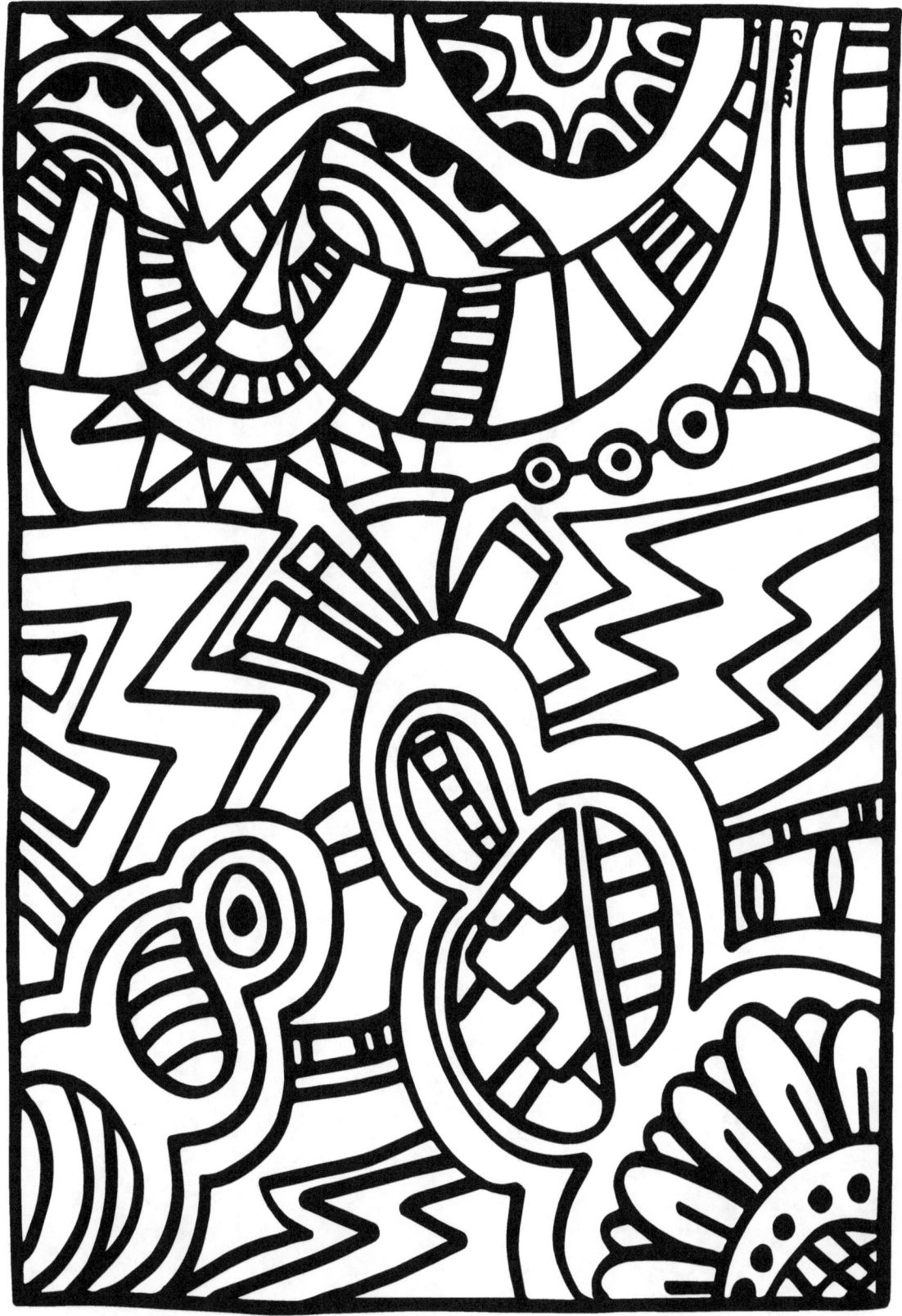

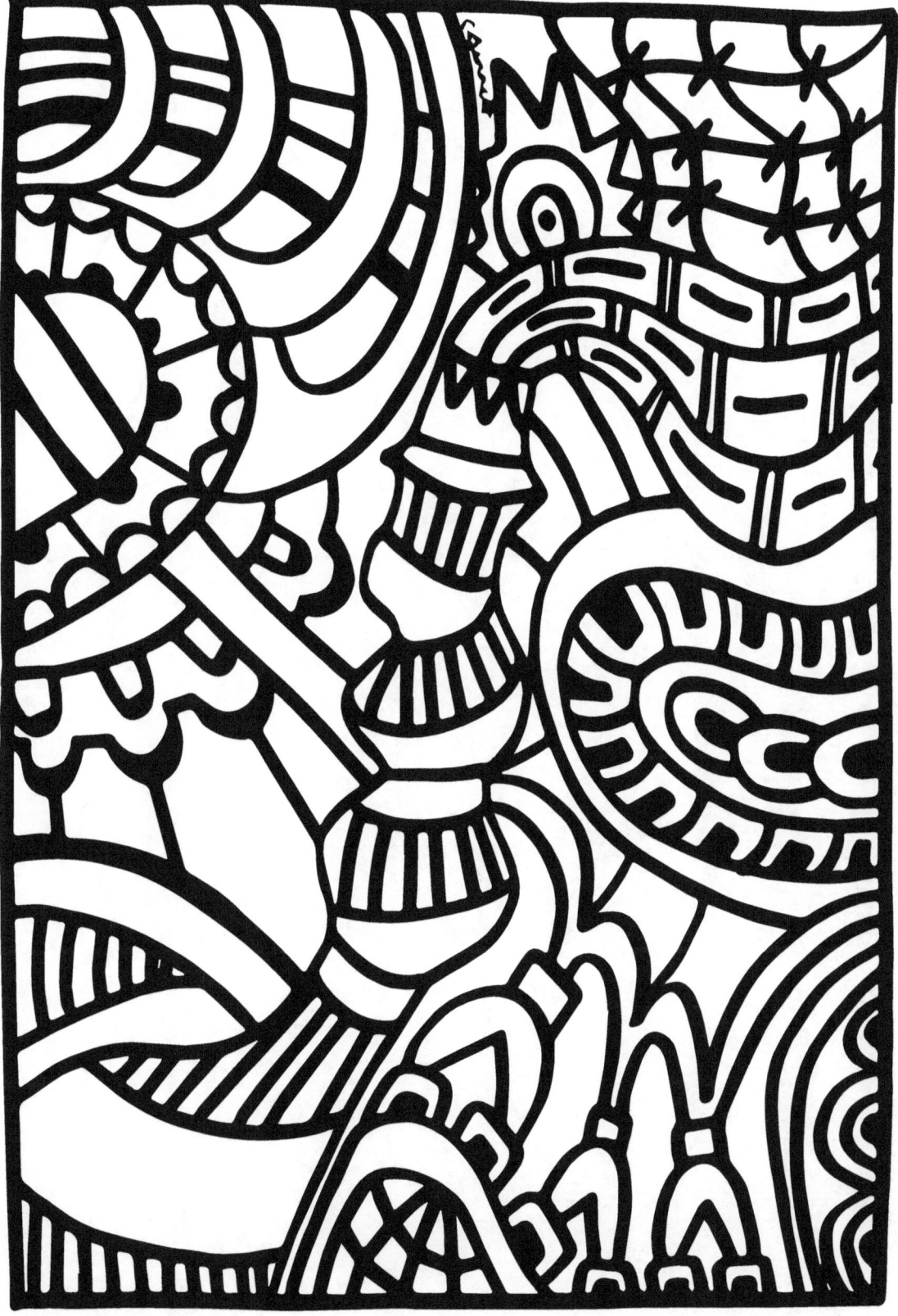

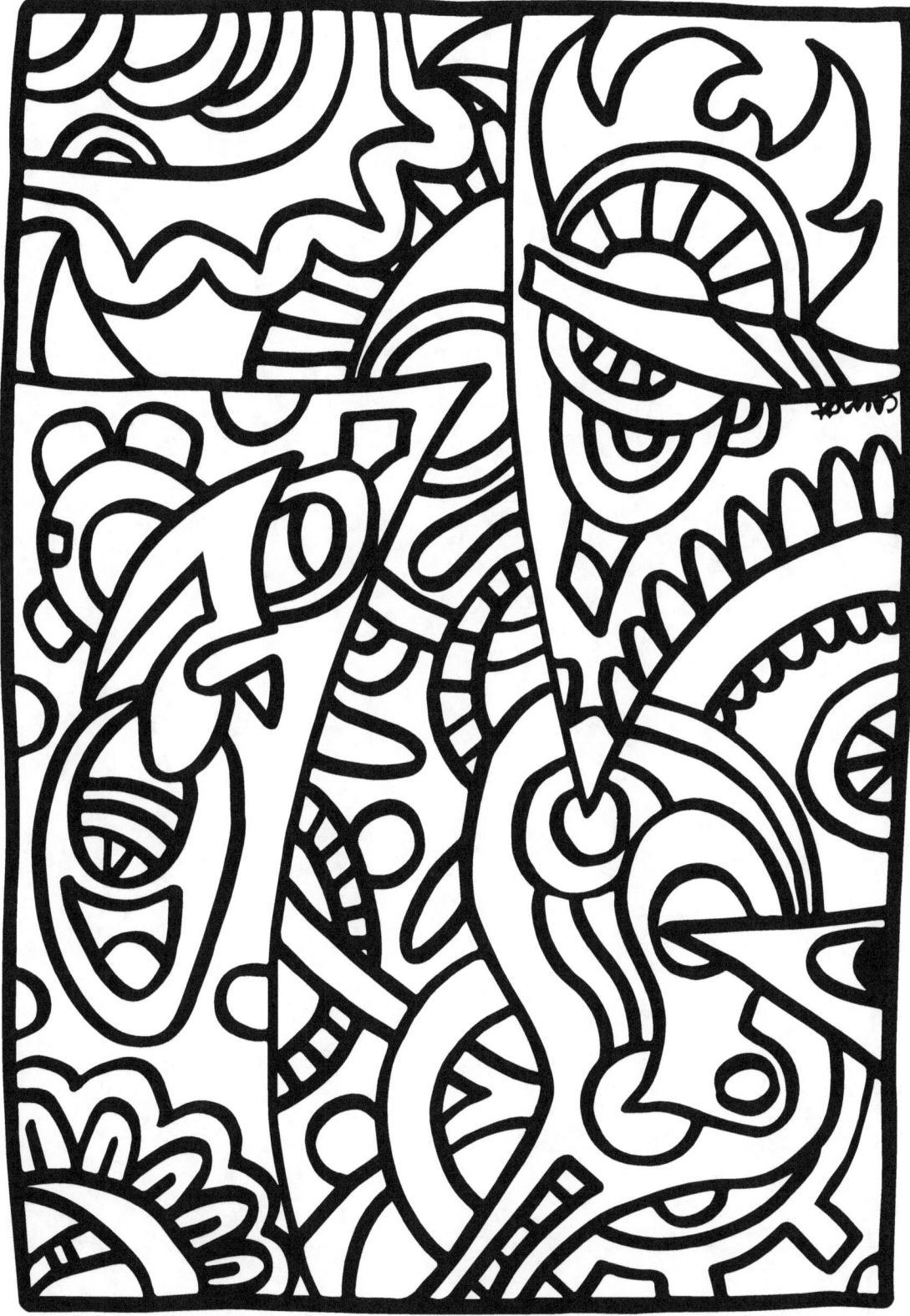

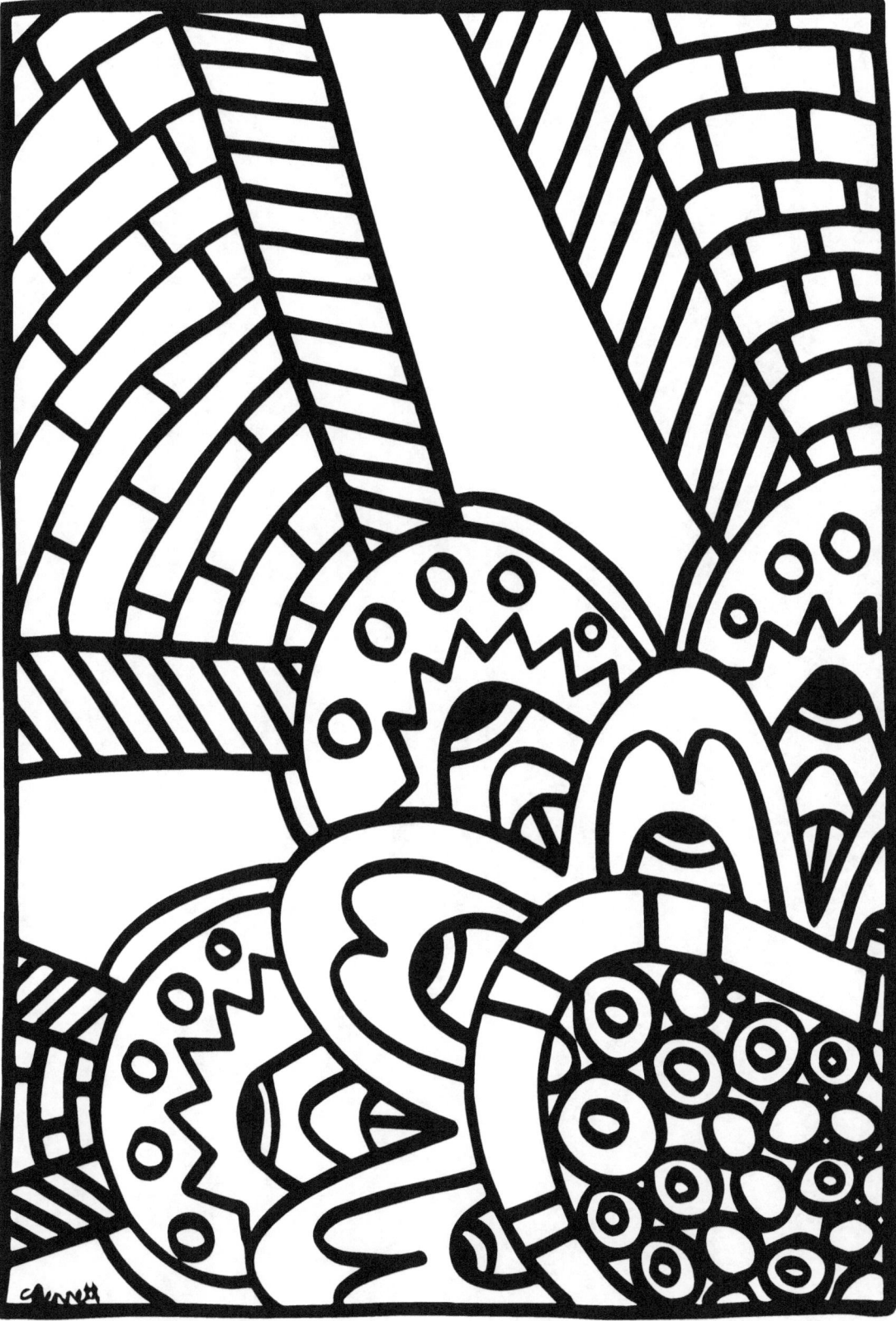

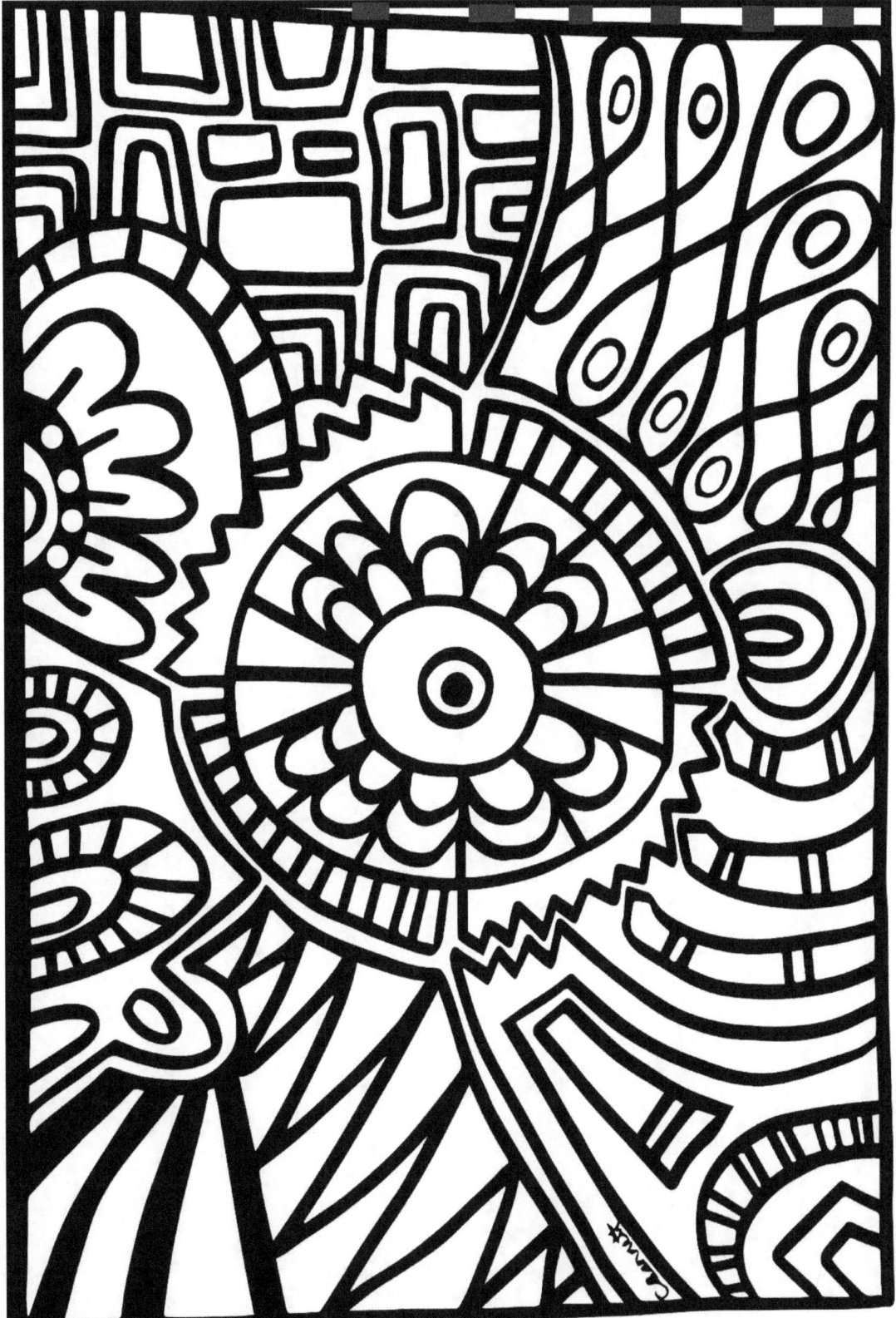

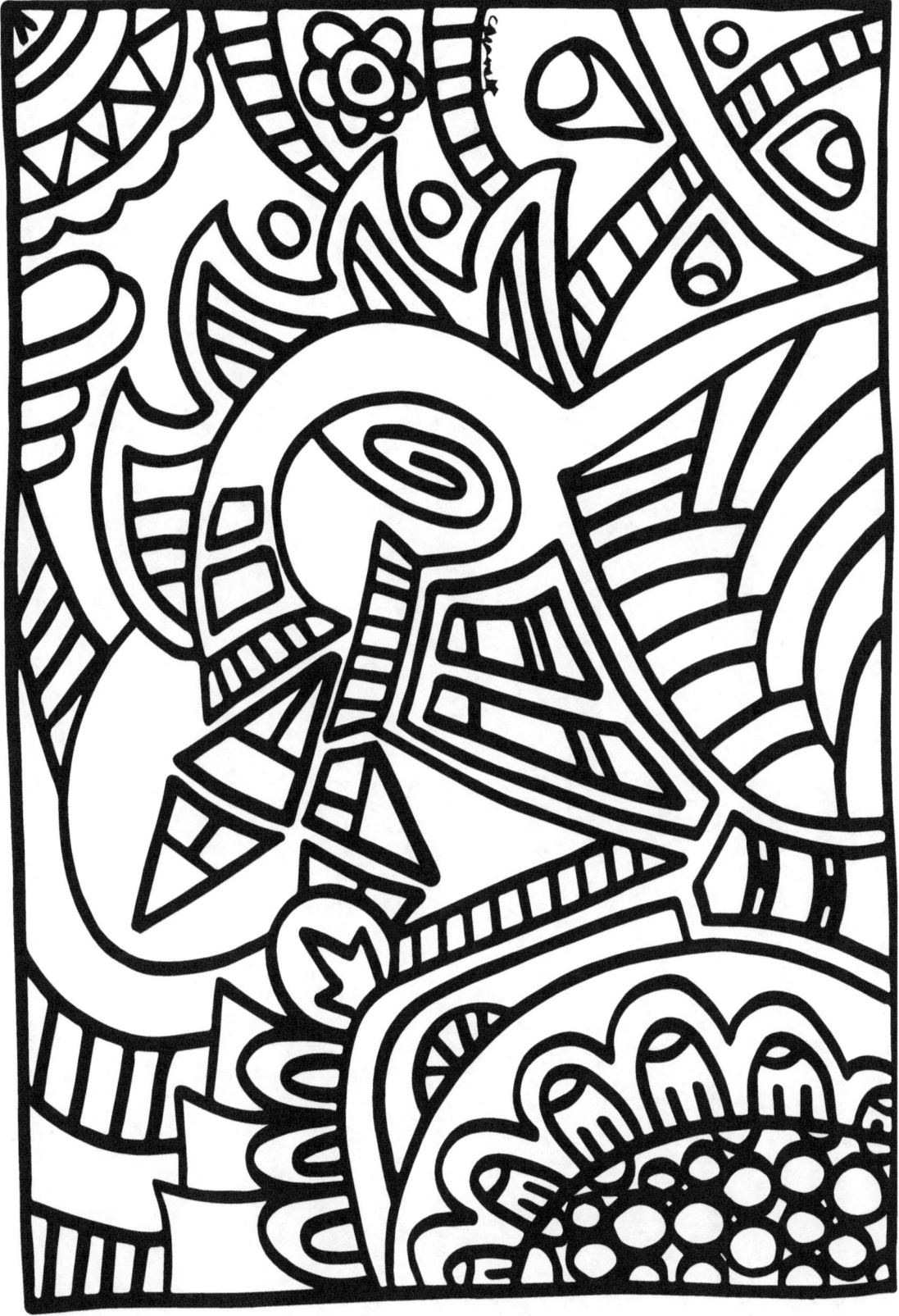

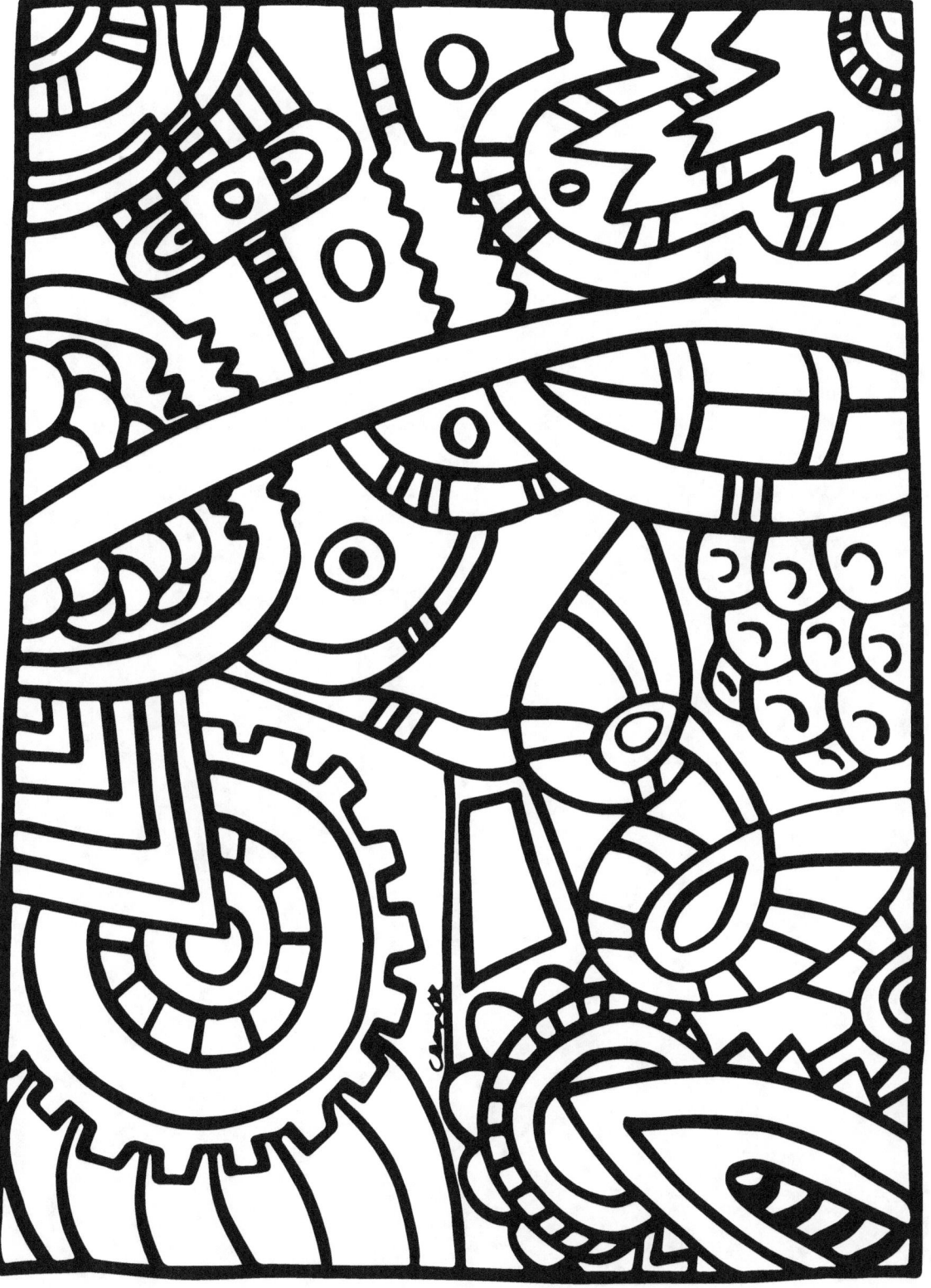

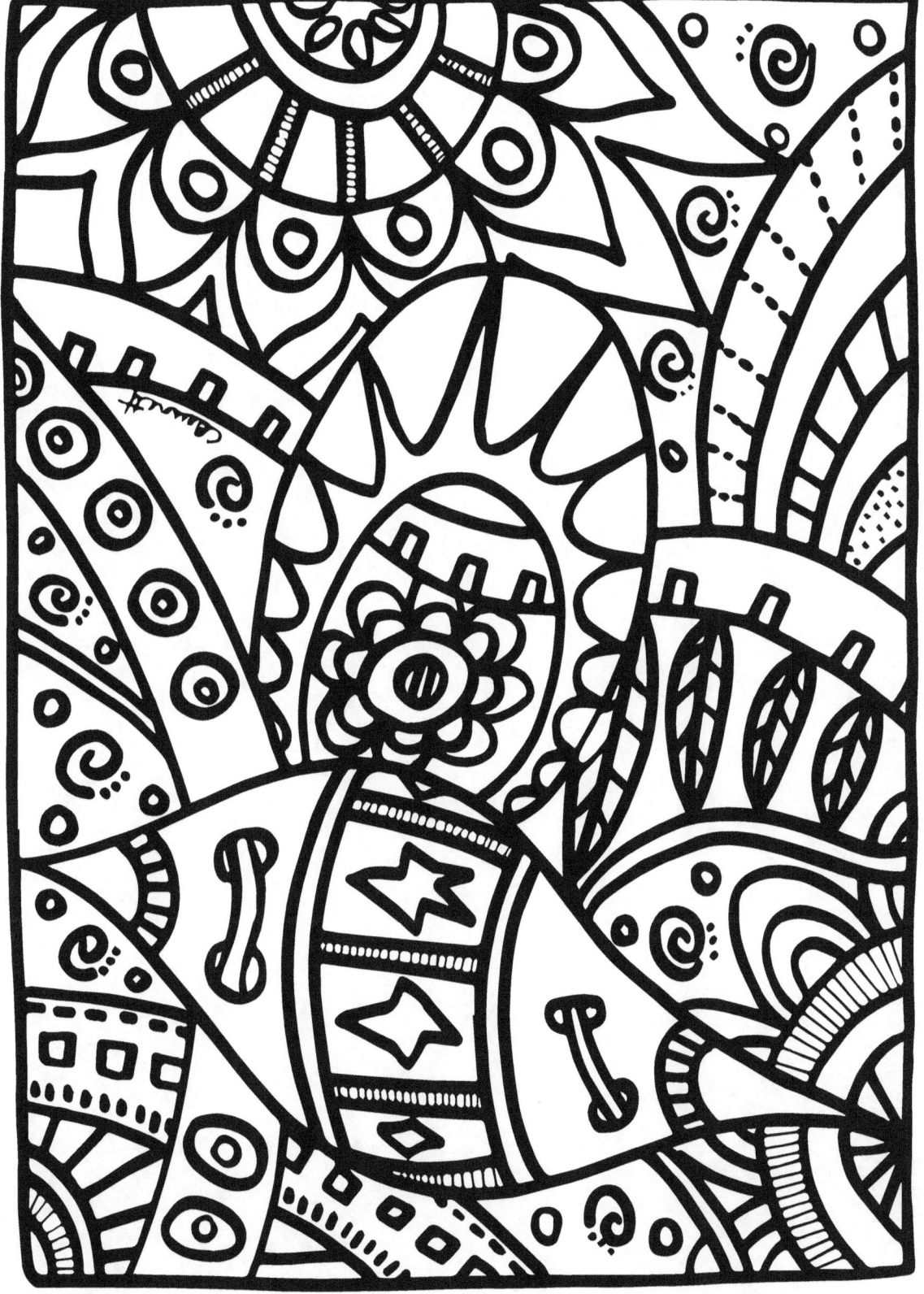

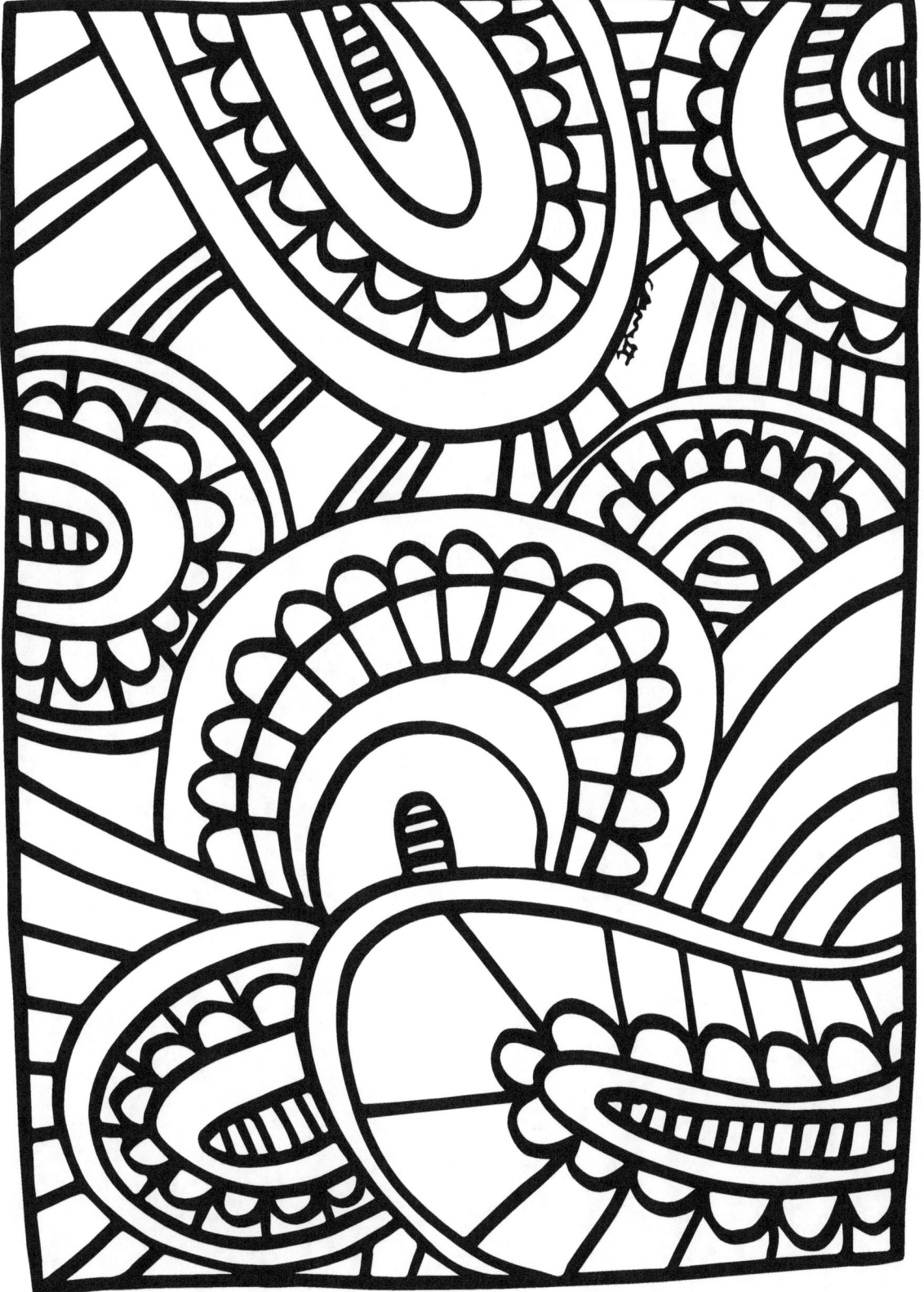

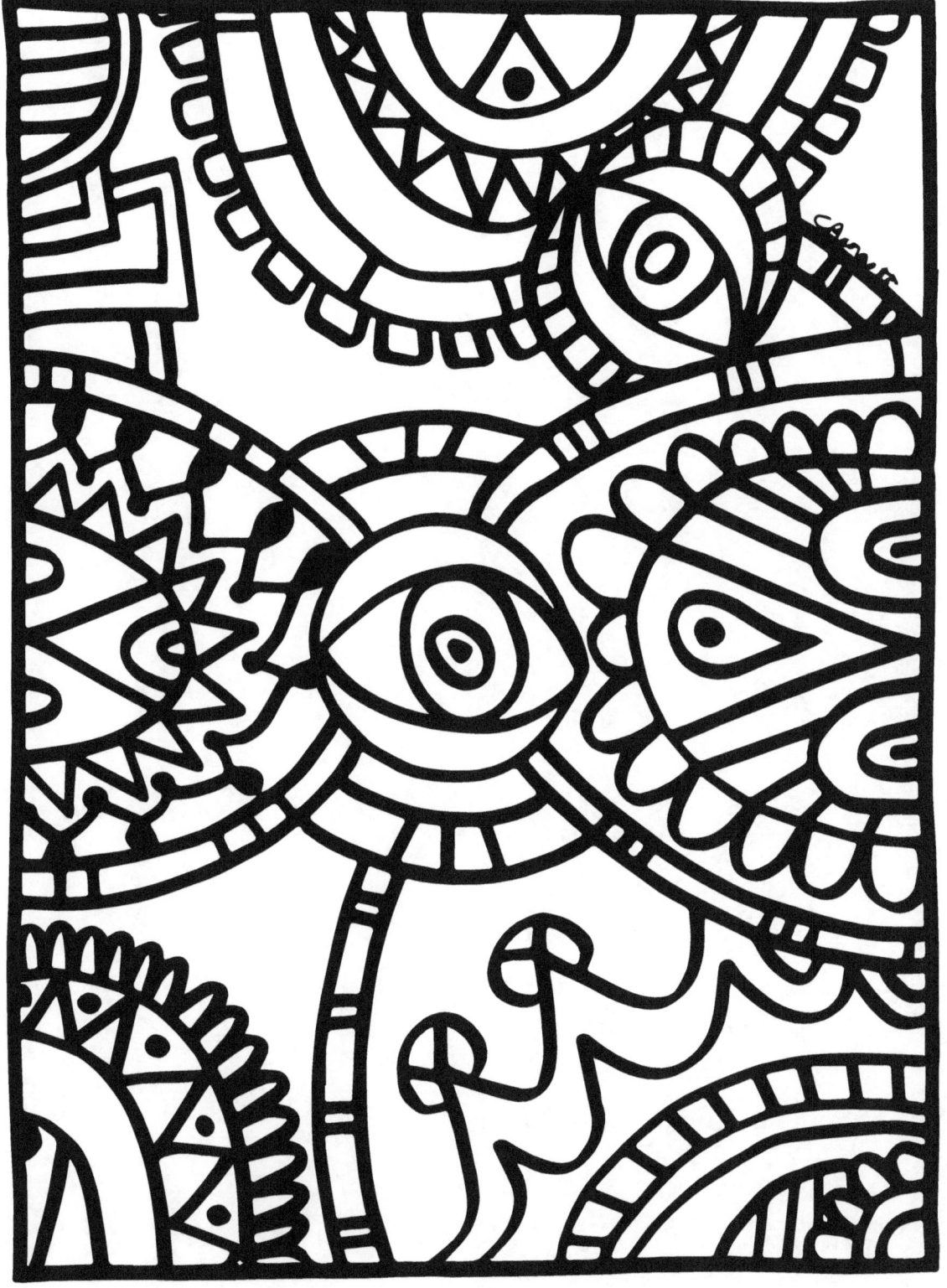

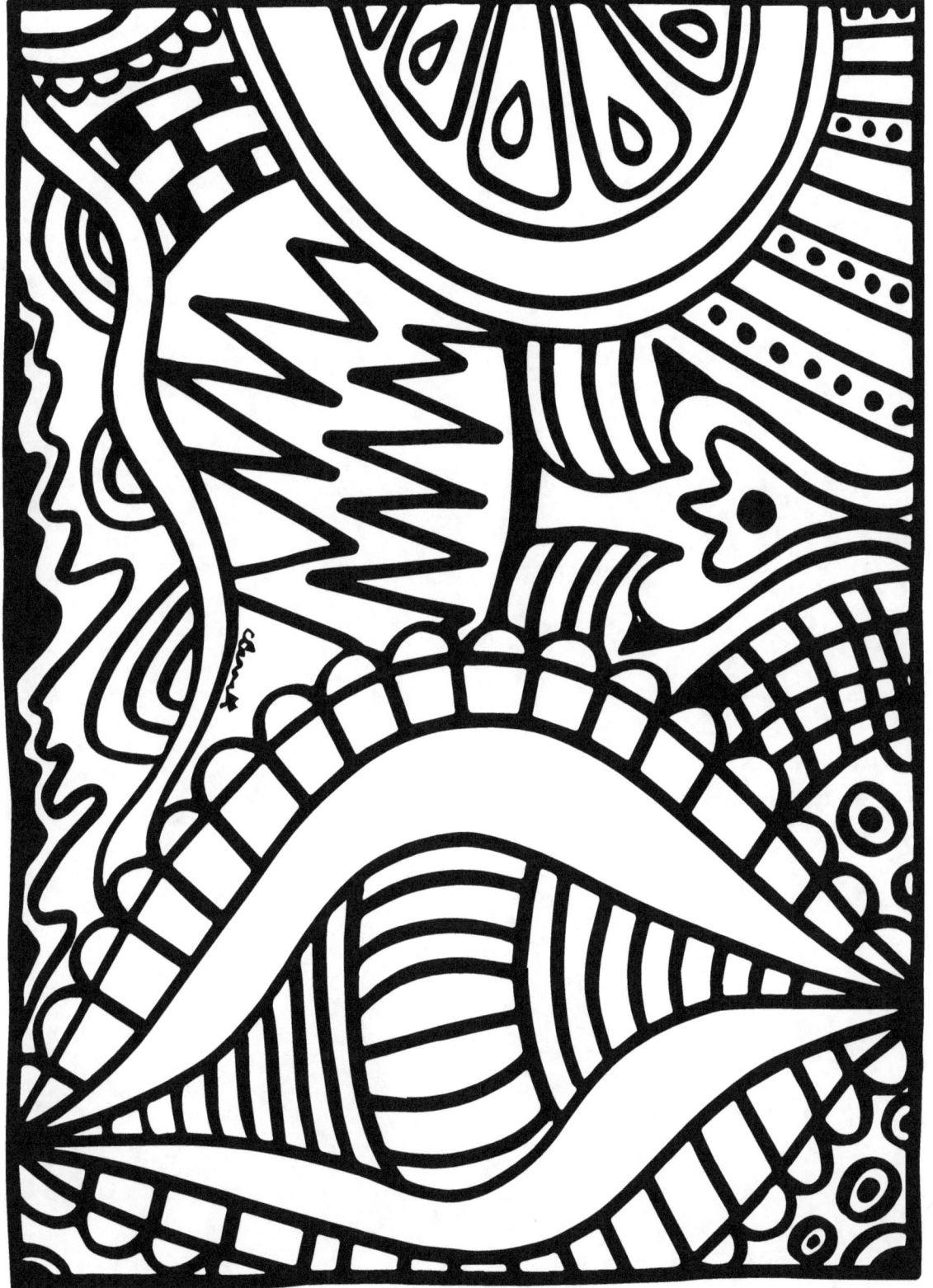

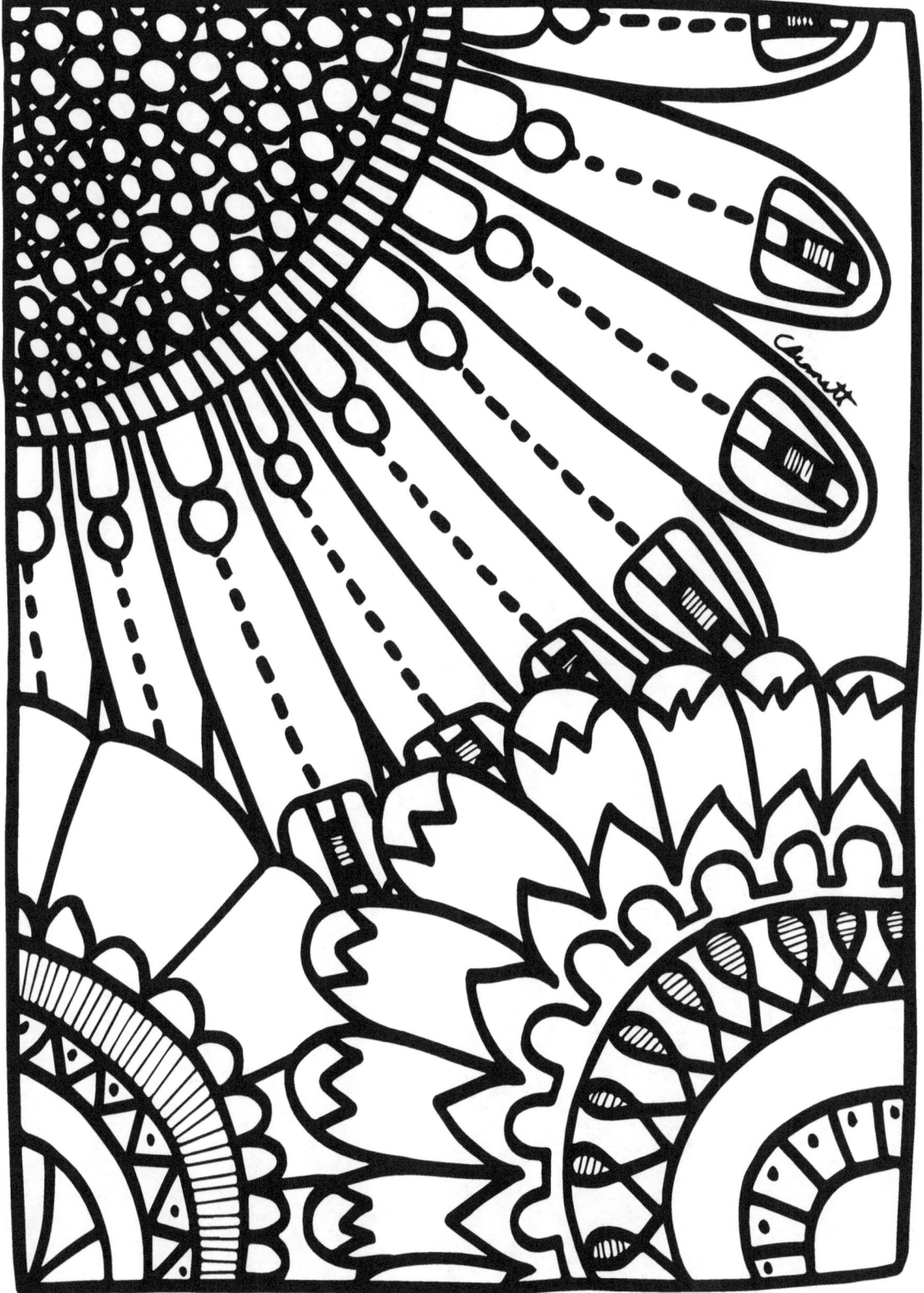

♥♥♥♥♥ Thank you Doodle Friends! ♥♥♥♥♥

This publication would NOT have been possible, if not for the support, encouragement and assistance of all my DOODLE FRIENDS!

Diane Bleck, I had no idea that tuning in to your Periscopes in 2015 would have brought me to this project. You enabled me to open my heart and unlock my creativity through doodling. I would never have realized this dream and this possibility without you and the DOODLE INSTITUTE. For that, I will be forever grateful.

Doodle Friends!!! There are too many of you to list. Your encouragement, inspiration and support have been incredible. You are some of the most awesome, creative and thoughtful virtual friends, a girl could ever ask for! I look forward to seeing you all continue to unlock your awesomeness. Right Muddy?

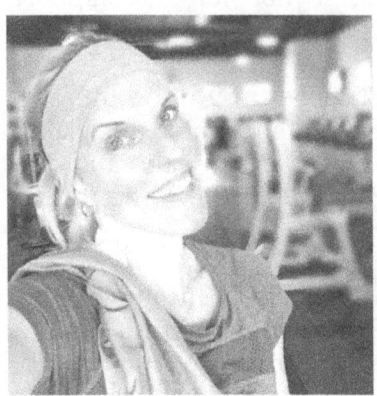

Christine Bennett is a fitness coach and certified Personal Trainer. She earned her B.A. from McMaster University, and MBA from the University of Central Arkansas.

After years of being in the corporate world, Christine found her passion in fitness and most recently, in doodling! This coloring book is an inspired combination of those passions.

Follow Christine on social media!

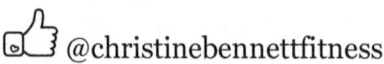 @christinebennettfitness

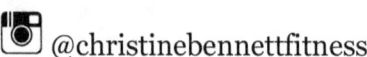 @christinebennettfitness